CW00685845

IAN MITCHELL DAVIDSON

A HERITAGE IN STONE

Characters and Conservation in North East Scotland

Foreword by Dame Evelyn Glennie

SANDSTONE PRESS
HIGHLAND | SCOTLAND

First published in Great Britain in 2017.
Sandstone Press Ltd
Dochcarty Road
Dingwall
Ross-shire
IV15 9UG
Scotland

www.sandstonepress.com

Editor: Alison Lang

The moral right of Ian Mitchell Davidson to be recognised as the author of this work has been asserted in accordance with the Copyright, Designs and Patents Act 1988.

The publisher acknowledges support from Creative Scotland towards publication of this volume.

The publisher acknowledges support from The National Trust for Scotland towards the publication of this volume.

ISBN: 978-1-910985-29-8

Jacket and book design by Heather Macpherson at Raspberry Creative Type, Edinburgh. Printed and bound by Pozkal, Poland.

CONTENTS

Acknowledgements   V
Foreword: Dame Evelyn Glennie   VI
Introduction   IX

1. A Cavalcade of Characters   1
2. Bill and the Unknown Craftsman   11
3. Communists, Kilts and Conferences   19
4. Weeping Stones and an Unpredictable Bulge   27
5. Ghosts   37
6. Fighting Butterflies   49
7. Offices, Shops and Railway Premises   59
8. Basil, the Bens and the Sphinx   67
9. Adam and the Happy Masons   77
10. First Nations   83
11. Strawberries and Peaches   89
12. The Aunties   95
13. Two Hills   103
14. An Estate in Ruins   111
15. The Rude Spout of Craigievar   119
16. True Grit   127
17. Pink Castle   137
18. The Prince and the Piper   147
19. The Old Tower   151
20. Damp Patch   159
21. King Robert's Throne   167
22. The Muckle Steen   175
23. Cushie Doo   179
24. Foghorn   183
25. Bang   187
26. Skirlie   195
27. Lowsin Time   199

Select bibliography   203
Useful websites   205
Glossary of architectural terms   206
References   207

For
Kim, Kate and Jamie

ACKNOWLEDGEMENTS

I would like to acknowledge all of my colleagues and, although it is not possible to thank everyone, the following deserve special mention. In particular, I am indebted to Bill Hanlin MBE, formerly assistant director and national buildings advisor for the Trust, who became my mentor for ten years before he retired in 1993. Bill was a kind and generous colleague who is much missed.

In addition, I would like to record a few names from those early years, and I hope those from more recent years will forgive me. I want to thank Mike Hunter, Dick and Jenny Hillson, Marjory Bennett, Flora Galloway, Sandy and Steve Le Gassick, Kitty Pawson, Andrew Robertson, Peter Chalmers, Richard Miller, Irene Durno, Rhona Jarvis, Robert Grant, Neal Sharp, Philip Schreiber, Alexander Bennett and many, many more.

Many thanks to Alison Lang, the editor, who took the ungrammatical and made it grammatical, the repetitive and made it readable, and the dull and made it interesting, to Jim Henderson for permission to use his superb photographs of Trust properties, to Heather Macpherson of Raspberry Creative Type for her beautiful design, and of course to everyone at Sandstone Press.

Above all, I thank my family, my wife Kim and our children Kate and Jamie, who have put up with my enthusiasms more than most.

Last, and by no means least, my grateful thanks go to a kind and generous supporter whose love for and commitment to so many of the properties in the care of the National Trust for Scotland have been inspirational. He knows who he is and will remain anonymous at his own wish.

All royalties from sales of this book will go to the National Trust for Scotland.

FOREWORD BY DAME EVELYN GLENNIE

I grew up on a farm on top of a windy hill in Aberdeenshire and I can remember feeling the sound of that wind on my face, drawing unbidden tears. The vibrations of the wind created sound through my whole being.

Farming the land can be a hard-won living, especially near Buchan, which sits in that shoulder of land that sticks out into the North Sea, pointing towards Scandinavia where its ancient trade links were forged. Just to the south lies the Garioch (pronounced Geery in the local Doric language) and here is Bennachie, the Fujisan of the county; its conical peak is the prow of the great Cairngorm mountain massif to the west.

The sea and the mountains frame the area, which has often seemed a place apart, being inconveniently distant from the population centres of Scotland's central belt.

The people and the landscape of my youth are one with each other, and I became aware at an early age of the rhythm of changing seasons and a love of music.

Music is a constant companion in the North East of Scotland. It has one of the richest traditions of song to be found anywhere and the ancient ballads are still sung today. The old men and women of my youth who might be persuaded to share their tunes with us are mostly gone now but their children and grandchildren have not forgotten them. The music of the North East remains a vibrant and living culture and is not insular. The Aberdeen International Youth Festival brings music and performance to so many from around the world each year.

As a young girl I was fortunate to enjoy a wonderful education at Cairnorrie, my local primary school, and in Ellon, performing regularly in the orchestra, and my teachers ensured that I had the grounding I needed to carry me onward.

Living near to that small market town, I soon became aware of the National Trust for Scotland, especially because the beautiful Haddo House was nearby, where a choir had been established that attracted the great musicians of their day, including Benjamin Britten, Ralph Vaughan Williams and Janet Baker. The local farmers and bank managers, ploughmen and shopkeepers would gather each week to sing the great choral works, always to the highest standards. It remains to this day an example of the professionalism that dedication and community can bring about.

Music is not the only gift offered here. Aberdeenshire is famous for many things—whisky, farming and castles to name but three.

Great houses like Haddo are special and the North East has so many. The castles of Mar are scattered around and several are in the care of the National Trust for Scotland. The Trust is a much-loved institution in Aberdeenshire and the greatest concentration of its members are clustered there. Over the past sixty or seventy years it has gathered in many of the places at greatest risk and opened them to those who want to visit. It has provided opportunities for employment and to develop expertise in conservation. Its work brings opportunities for local craftsmen and women to develop skills and take those skills into the wider environment, enriching everyone.

I know that these places can only survive thanks to the people who care for them—the small army of cleaners, gardeners, masons and painters, the surveyors and managers, archaeologists and curators. These dedicated people are unseen, and I am pleased to welcome a book that celebrates their achievements and perhaps introduces new places to readers who may one day visit.

The author married into the local farming community, meeting his wife at Fyvie Castle where she was a guide on a summer's employment in a break from university. She and I played in that school orchestra together and have been friends for life. Ian spent most of his career with the Trust In many different roles throughout the organisation. He has travelled the world as a speaker on conservation and is now a visiting professor at Robert Gordon University and a heritage consultant. I know that he loved his time with the Trust and especially the people he worked with who are his friends.

Evelyn Glennie CH, DBE
London
2017

INTRODUCTION

These stories emerged from thirty years with the National Trust for Scotland, mostly as a surveyor but at times something else. That's a long time and I can be forgetful, which means that while everything that you read actually happened, it's not necessarily in chronological order or epistemologically accurate so I place my apologies here at the beginning of my attempt at recording some of the anecdotes that colleagues have had to suffer over the years. I hope they are interesting and if they are informative too, so much the better. Mostly these tales are about people that I have known, and I hope that the stories they gave me are an insight into the past that suggests the way things can change but also remain the same.

Castles can seem immovable, ancient and unchanging, and in Scotland there are thousands, scattered across the whole of the nation. Some are now nothing more than a pile of stones, or 'rickle o steens' as they might be described in the local Doric language, while others stand on volcanic rocks, beckoning visitors. Their image is powerful, but only because of an army of men and women who have lived, died, cleaned, repaired and cared for them.

Aberdeenshire has the greatest concentration of these places, with a castle, it sometimes appears, three miles from you wherever you might stand. Most will be nothing more than bumps on the ground, while others may have seen Robert the Bruce visit or the Covenanters battle or perhaps wounded soldiers convalesce from the trenches of World War I.

The stories that follow may be unreliable because they have been drawn from memory, that most fragile of containers, but I hope that the fragility has retained the essence of those people I have walked beside and that these stories do them honour. The unknown craftsman is an acknowledged character but it is rare that such artisans are given life beyond their prosaic existence. Together they have moved mountains, and I hope that this collection shines a dim light on them.

In many ways I am not really a surveyor, which has been in my job title more often than not. I think it would be more reasonable to call me something else and I leave that to others to judge, but I have been involved with Scotland's cultural and natural heritage for almost my entire career, mostly in the North East of Scotland, where I have tried to ensure, with my colleagues, that the heritage of Aberdeenshire, Angus, Perthshire and the Cairngorms is passed on to future generations 'in the full richness of

Bennachie (Jim Henderson)

Soldiers convalescing at Leith Hall, 1914-1918

its authenticity', to quote the Venice Charter[1]. This approach to the environment would have remained invisible to me were it not for the National Trust for Scotland and the on-going education I have enjoyed. My initial training did not equip me for this experience, and I am not alone in that.

That training took place in Glasgow, where I was born and where I lived until I moved to work for the Trust in Aberdeenshire, and I was pretty much unaware of this cold corner of North-East Scotland until I arrived in 1983. This is not unusual. Aberdeenshire has always been a place apart. Today, despite the efforts of the marketeers, as they are called, the great draws for visitors to Scotland remain the Loch Ness monster, the much photographed castles on the islands and the Edinburgh Festival. At times there seems to have been unwillingness on the part of the politicians to celebrate our rural heritage; they have championed instead the urban and cosmopolitan nature of the big cities. Scotland's cities are worthy of the recognition, but we cannot escape our past and the value that visitors and inhabitants place on it, nor the role it plays in our lives today, anchoring people to the place and committing them to its improvement.

Aberdeenshire is often bypassed by visitors who seek the romance of the hills and islands. It is inconveniently distant from the capital and throughout the years its farming and fishing communities had a self-sufficiency that sustained them without much assistance from elsewhere. This created a close community, which has recently seen an influx of new people, drawn by the discovery of oil just off the coast. Over the last forty years or so you could meet someone from almost any country in the world walking through the small market towns, and as an 'inabootcomer' myself I know that they have been welcomed with open arms.

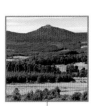

Anyone who looks at the more recent patterns of migration over the last twenty years or so and has an eye to the past will find it of great interest to see the arrival of Eastern Europeans from Poland and the Baltic countries. It seems as if the ancient trading links from Aberdeen to Danzig, Tallinn and Riga are being re-established, though the recent insularity of the 'Brexit' decision has placed this at risk. If you were to go to the most iconic of the Aberdeenshire castles, Craigievar, you would find wooden panels and boards that were hewn from the great pine trees that once grew in those lands in the sixteenth century, imported by the laird known as Danzig Willie. The languages of northern Europe would have been well known to him through his use of the Doric dialect, which today still has embedded within it many remnants of that vocabulary.

This collection of stories is an attempt to give a flavour of how one person experienced this history and those changes. It tries to demonstrate how the conservation community uses its skills to protect this resource and the challenges it faces. I have attempted to provide a narrative rather than a chronological flow and therefore I have taken liberties with some timelines and have attributed some of the experiences to individuals to offer a narrative that I hope is true, at least in its colour. As I gathered the stories

Subtle repairs to pine flooring at Crathes (Ian M Davidson)

J. M. Barrie sitting on the settle in his London home

for my colleagues it was clear that any attempt to offer a 'this followed that' narrative was destined to bore the reader. I therefore apologise here if anyone sees inaccuracies that put a point of view that they do not agree with. The tales are my own and have been filtered and reviewed through retelling to what they now are.

The National Trust for Scotland is unique. It is the only body that takes a truly holistic approach to conserving our heritage, both tangible and intangible. I prefer the term 'conservation' to 'preservation', which sounds like pickling to me. Conservation is about managing change, not preventing it.

There is a good example of the holistic approach to conservation in the birthplace of J. M. Barrie, playwright and author of *Peter Pan*. In a weaver's cottage in Kirriemuir you can visit the rooms where he lived as a child.

In many ways a birthplace museum is a very challenging place to conserve. Some might say that the least interesting thing Barrie did was be born. There are now few of the original artefacts from those early years, though those that remain give a slight but tangible glimpse into his origins, so how do you conserve and display such a space to engage a visitor?

For me, the most significant part of the place lies in the intangible story of how his mother grieved at the loss of his brother, who died in 1867 a week after hitting his head and fracturing his skull in an accident on a skating pond, and how Barrie sat on the stair, apparently an unloved infant, wondering why he was rejected and why his brother would never grow up.

The unique quality of the Trust is to hold this intangible heritage while at the same time attempting elsewhere the restoration of the ancient pine forest in the Cairngorms or displaying masterpieces of fine art in great country houses. I have been fortunate enough to see some of this at first hand.

Margaret Ogilvy, J. M . Barrie's mother

Peter Pan costumes in Barrie's birthplace

The Trust is not a paragon and at times it fails, but more often it succeeds, sometimes to its own bemusement. A major piece of work can take decades to implement and these stories try to give an insight to how a vision for conservation can be delivered despite changes in personnel and priorities over such a long period.

The following tales were written to amuse and inform colleagues and friends, who are, I think, less fortunate

Barrie's crib

than me, since I knew the last generation that worked with the horse and used traditional materials daily, with skills that now pass into history.

1

A CAVALCADE OF CHARACTERS

Eric the plasterer preferred to work alone and could be quite elusive. Despite his foibles, he was always in great demand in the Garioch because he could make cornices better than anyone.

He came to Haddo House in 1985, running new cornices in a room on the ground floor, but only after I had spent months fruitlessly searching for him. Weeks passed and my letters went unanswered, phone calls would not be returned and doorbells were ignored. Then one day Eric arrived, his hair tousled, dungarees stained and smeared with plaster and paint, with bleary eyes that suggested a hard weekend. When he opened the back of his white van, he took out immaculate tools and worked without a break, focusing on the task in hand, and creating a beautiful object.

Eric was not unusual, other than in his individual foibles; there were many craftsmen at the time that a young surveyor might call on, but plasterers were scarce.

We spoke about the ancient plaster decoration at Craigievar Castle, an hour's drive away, where a team of men like Eric would have toiled in the 1600s.

Craigievar's ornate ceilings were created by itinerant plasterers, and if you know where to look you will see that some are not quite perfect. Eric's forebears must have found it a cold place to work and far from home. It's hardly surprising if they pushed a little too quickly to get things finished and maybe escape before the return of Willie Forbes, the laird at the time, known by the title 'Maister' in reference to his university degree.

Imagine those plasterers sitting in their cart, making their way day after day over rutted tracks deep into Strathdon before finally reaching the hill where an old tower house was being improved. The masons had practically demolished the old place, creating a fantasy of turrets and gables up at the roof and a suite of rooms to meet the Maister's new aspiration to elegance. It is not hard to picture these craftsmen stepping over boards and broken stones into the yard, no doubt complaining that things should be more advanced and that they shouldn't be expected to work in such a mess.

They would set up a shed in the mud where the stonemasons had been, before mixing the lime, sand and horsehair and applying it to the new ceilings. The lime had

William 'Danzig Willie' Forbes of Menie and Craigievar (1566-1627) by George Jamieson to be mature, so their burned limestone was slaked in water, turning the quicklime or calcium oxide into calcium hydroxide, and the resulting putty was left to age in barrels. The sand could have come out of the river nearby and the hair would have been horsehair, probably from the tail for length and strength. Their ponies would have looked a little short at the back when the supplies ran out.

One day as Eric laboured at Haddo and I watched him run the mould along the new cornice, a phone call came through from Johnnie Morgan, the joiner over at Craigievar. I had to leave Eric and rush to Craigievar. One of the ceilings was about to collapse.

The first cracks had appeared ten years earlier, in 1975, in the Blue Room just below the Long Gallery, and the Trust had commissioned its consultant architect, Schomberg Scott, to fix them.

Schomberg Scott had retired in 1979, but Johnnie described him to me as a wiry, short-fused architect who liked leaping up ladders. I had heard of him. He had been the dominant historic buildings architect in Scotland and worked at most of the Trust properties in Aberdeenshire. In 1966, for example, he repaired Crathes Castle after a catastrophic fire, and over at Pitmedden he designed the gates at the Great Garden and even hand-made tapestry for the chairs himself at Leith Hall. Also, to the relief of thousands, the public toilets at Craigievar were built to his design in the early 1970s.

Those first cracks were found by Raeburn Murray, the tiny and fearsome manager, who took up the cause. Soon Schomberg was there and when he finished he wrote a brief report stating that, apart from the Blue Room, there were no other cracks to be seen. That was in 1978. Unfortunately, just a few years later there were many more cracks throughout the building and Raeburn, with Schomberg now gone, had nowhere to turn for help.

Then to her surprise, on a spring morning in 1983, an old Ford Cortina rolled up to the front door, making a mess of the finely raked gravel. I stepped up to the great door, lifted the silvery knocker and rapped loudly, as I had been advised. Raeburn, who exhibited similar characteristics to a rod of iron, answered. Her sharp little eyes stared fiercely from under her neatly combed short grey hair. Her serious expression was fitting for a custodian who sought to protect the castle from anyone who might wish to change anything.

Crathes Castle after the fire of 1966

Our first encounter was not auspicious. 'How did you get here?' Her thin smile did not reassure me.

'Through Alford,' I replied, pronouncing the 'L' and pleased to have found the place without getting lost on the way.

Raeburn bristled. 'Aff-rd, you mean,' and I was put in my place, never having heard the word pronounced. I knew by then that Garioch was pronounced 'Geery', but clearly I had more to learn about Aberdeenshire place names. I felt sheepish as she let me in.

A few months later, I thought I had made a breakthrough in our relationship. I was investigating some minor problem when she appeared and said kindly, 'I've been making soup. Would you like to come up to the cottage for a bowl at lunchtime?'

I was a delighted that we were getting on so well. 'Oh, yes please,' I said.

'Come up at one,' she said. I made sure that I arrived on time.

Raeburn spent each summer in the steading cottage at the back of the castle. The door is placed within a tiny courtyard floored with river-washed setts. I approached timidly and rang the bell. It opened, a bowl was handed out and the door was closed. I stood there, a little forlorn, and enjoyed the broth. Fortunately it was summer and not raining.

Raeburn was not rude. She was tough, independent and an artist who could often be seen sketching with her watercolours nearby. I grew to respect her enormously for the wonderful care she took of the place, and so did the guides, many of whom had been there for years.

Raeburn's cottage

Raeburn retired in 1984 and she passed away, in her nineties, in 2014.

On that first visit, as the ice melted in her eyes, I was given a tour around the castle and taken to see the cracks in the Queen's Room, housekeeper's room and schoolroom. Raeburn asked, 'What do you think of these, hmmm?' She looked quizzically up at me as we gazed, deciding whether I was any use at all. 'These cracks are new.' There was a hint of suppressed ferocity in her tone; she was an Edinburgh matriarch who was weighing my reaction in the balance. Johnnie's steady and unhurried placid tone in that call sometime later was less challenging.

The schoolroom had the most recent ceiling. Raeburn told me that it had been replaced about a hundred years earlier when its predecessor had fallen down. This was, she said with a straight face, due to bouncing from the floor above, 'The maid's bedroom.'

Raeburn worked at Craigievar in the summer months but the groundsman was there all year, with his wife, the part-time cleaner. Geordie was yet another in the cavalcade of characters that made the Trust such a delight. Even more were to follow.

Geordie was typical of the hardworking Trust handymen of the time. He had been a farm labourer, with Doric as his first tongue, and was never without his tweed bunnet. Bunnets come in two kinds, with or without an elasticated patch at the back to keep them in place. The working man tended to go for that, whereas the tweedy lairds did not need such practicality. It's a way for the gent to demonstrate that he does not need to bend over to pick something up when there are staff to do it.

Only once did I note Geordie's bald crown and I pointed it out with as little tact as I could muster. 'Aye,' Geordie replied with a salacious grin. 'Aye, that's fae pushing the wife up the stairs.'

Each winter Raeburn would return to Edinburgh, and Geordie and Mrs Geordie looked after the castle. This consisted mainly of laying traps for mice and sweeping snow off the viewing platforms. They also let in tradesmen and the cleaner.

That first winter I would pop over from time to time. 'We'll take a wander up tae see Mrs Russell,' said Geordie and we went in to the castle. 'She's gey old these days,' he peched, struggling for breath as we climbed up. 'She's in her eighties, mind, so she only does the brass polishing.'

'Oh,' I said, not knowing how to react.

'Aye,' he went on. 'I have to ging down the hill to pick her up most mornings noo.'

'Where does she stay?' I asked.

'It's yon hoosie over there,' he said, pointing through a window to a cottage at the bottom of the hill.

We found her right at the top of the tower. Mrs Russell sat at a table, cloth in hand. 'I see you live down there,' I said. It was the home she had shared with her late husband all her married life. Mary Russell was a cheerful kindly auld buddie, and she reminded me a little of my old Granny.

Her husband had been the parkman, or farm servant, for the laird at the time, Lord Sempill, and his wife. 'Ken this,' Mrs Russell said. 'The Lady would often have me gaither reeds for the floor.' I looked quizzical. 'She liked the smell and thought it made the place mair homely.'

Cecilia, Lady Sempill, who had wanted her to collect those rushes, was an important figure in the London art scene during the interwar years. She was a sculptor in her own right and a close friend of many of the great artists of the day.

I commented to Geordie

Mrs Mary Russell (Jim Henderson)

how lucky the castle was to still have Mrs Russell and how remarkable she was. 'Aye, you're richt,' says Geordie, 'but you should meet her mither.' I wondered if I had heard him correctly. 'Well,' he said, 'she's just hid to move over tae Alford for a sheltered house, now she's a hundred and six. Mrs Russell's no so happy about it. It means a bus trip to see her.'

The other grand lady, Lady Sempill, died in the early 1980s, nineteen years or so after her husband. She had lived, latterly, in a small cottage on the estate when she visited. Sadly, I never met her, but Raeburn protected the memory of her presence in the castle and this was the steel I encountered that first day.

Raeburn ensured that the artistry in the placing of studio pottery by Bernard Leach, Lucie Rie and Hans Coper remained an echo of those days in London. Along with the rushes in the kitchen, the rooms had been lit by candles with fires burning in the hearth of the Great Hall. It must have been an enchanted place to grow up, like inhabiting a fairy tale or a dolls' house.

Cecilia Sempill's funeral mass was held in the Great Hall of the castle with her coffin resting on the merchants table in the middle of the room.

About ten years later, I met her brother-in-law, auld Sir Ewan, once the local doctor and well liked. A very interesting book could be written about him but I will restrict myself to a short tale. He was invited to take the salute when the Lonach pipe band came to beat the retreat at the castle. The invited guests included local landowners, dressed in their old family kilts, farmers with red faces and tight-fitting tweed jackets and a scattering of oil executives from Aberdeen in pinstripes. It was a fine, colourful affair.

We retired to the Great Hall where the fire was crackling and Sir Ewan, who now walked with the aid of two sticks, was placed on the wing-backed tartan armchair beside it. We all crowded in and Sir Ewan was asked to give a short address. He struggled to his feet and, in his ancient Forbes tartan kilt, thanked those there for attending and for the care the Trust took of the castle. Then he lamented the change in family fortunes, blaming this on the move from staunch Protestantism to Catholicism. His voice was

Sir Ewan Forbes of Craigievar and Brux (centre) with the author (left)

raised and his fist thumped the table. He had had the Kirk minister exorcise that Catholic funeral mass, he told us. The oil executives looked bewildered, but for me it was a window into 300 years of history, to the Covenanters and the arrival of the Marquis of Montrose at Bridge of Alford ready to do battle.

Life was not all tartan and stories as the 1980s rolled by, and I had not forgotten that phone call from Johnnie Morgan and the cracks on the ceilings. The years that intervened had been ones in which to monitor and learn. When Eric had been working at Haddo I had asked Johnnie, the Trust joiner, to repair some windows at Craigievar, in the room where Schomberg had done his repairs. He was working away, probably humming a tune in his quavering baritone voice, when Mrs Russell, stepped on to the floor in the room above, in a little turret. Johnnie looked up and saw the ceiling quiver, like a bowl of milky blancmange held upside down. He stepped swiftly out of the way, and got on the phone to me.

An hour or so later, I parked, this time off the gravel, found Johnnie and climbed up to the turret. Together we had a look under the floor above the ceiling, and found that the timber lath holding the plaster up was so badly decayed that it was no longer there. The ceiling was staying in place out of habit, held by the thin strands of horsehair binding it.

A while later I realised that the problem was caused by the cement harling that had been applied to the castle walls in 1973 and which was now forcing water into the building. I set to work designing a repair for the plaster, knowing that the cement would have to come off one day. Reharling was needed, but it would be expensive.

I repaired the turret with Johnnie, and fortunately the plaster stayed in place so Eric was not needed, but I took a closer look at the other cracks Raeburn had pointed out and realised that major repairs were needed on all of them. After much scratching of heads and sucking of teeth it was clear there were two problems causing those cracks. The first was that the water had rotted some of the lath, as we had found with that turret. The other was that Craigievar had become very popular, and the tramping feet of guided tours thumping across the floors every twenty minutes in the afternoon had been too much.

As I examined each ceiling, I was drawn to the housekeeper's room. For those with a passing knowledge of the place, that is the room with the bath in the box bed. When the tour guide arrived in the room above they would walk in first and the visitors would follow. It is a small room and they would gather in a row just inside the door, all standing over a single joist, to hear the story. The ceiling below cracked under the weight.

The floorboards that should have spread the load over several joists were 'butt jointed' on that joist, which meant they did not spread the load very efficiently. They appeared to be cut from a single tree, wide at one end and narrow at the other and laid alternately. They could not be lifted without unacceptable damage. Fortunately, a small repair had left a patch of newer flooring, which allowed us to add some strength to take the load of the chorus line of visitors.

Cornice about to fall away in the Queen's Room

Craigievar ceiling crack seen from above

Fixing these cracks was going to be too big a job for Johnnie on his own and it was at this time that I met and worked alongside Ian Masson and his son David, from Garlogie a few miles away. Their skill saved these ceilings.

A cornice in the Queen's Room was about to fall away, and the Massons and I set about keeping it there. As Ian and David worked away, we became aware of a quiet squeaking from behind the panels by the window. It would start when work began and stop when there was quiet. We realised that bats had probably made their way in through the roof and down behind the panels to where it was warm. They did not seem perturbed at all by this activity and were still squeaking when the work was done and the craftsmen had left.

Soon the cornice was repaired and we redecorated the ceiling with a lime wash, made on site especially for the job. Another local craftsman, Ally, came to our aid. Ally was blunt spoken, but he and his brother Graeme were masters of their craft. They took on the challenge and together got the paint ready and onto the ceiling.

Lime wash has a lot of water in it and you must apply many coats to get the desired effect. Ally and his team worked hard and when they were finished it looked great, but a few days later he called me to say there was a problem. Brown stains had appeared on the repaired cornice.

I arrived in some trepidation but was relieved to find that the stain was from candle smoke that had been absorbed in this part of the ceiling, above the bed. Ally, however, was perturbed. 'Ye canna leave it like that, loon.' It took a bit of persuasion, but he eventually agreed to leave it.

Johnnie Morgan waxing the doors
at Craigievar

Queen's Room smoke stains

Crathes gallery ceiling: spot the plywood

Ally and his brother were great champions of traditional painting techniques and were sign-writers in the Victorian tradition. Their skill in 'graining' timber was almost mystical. Graining is a painted effect, replicating the look of timber. Usually it is not hard to tell this apart from the real thing but Ally and Graeme were artists at heart and had studied the different types of wood used in historic buildings and expanded their painters' art to mimic them.

I put their skills to the test over at Crathes, in the Long Gallery where the ceiling is covered by quarter-cut oak boards, a technique used to maximise the pattern effect of the grain. One of the panels had been replaced with plywood decades earlier. I asked Ally to grain this panel to match the rest and it has been a game of mine to challenge people to try to spot it. No one has.

What of Eric? After his work on the Haddo cornices was completed, he disappeared from view. We never met again.

Scotland's oldest field sport trophy

2

BILL AND THE UNKNOWN CRAFTSMAN

Bill seemed old and he would have been about fifty-five when we met in 1983. That's ancient when you are twenty-three.

He was the area surveyor and he knew I had arrived from Glasgow, where I had worked on the tenements, but he probably didn't know the awful things I did to them in the early 1980s. Looking back from the same 55th parallel that Bill occupied, I console myself that we were all learning about conservation. The Glasgow style was not Bill's style. The screaming rush and unforgiving attack on the historic buildings was not Bill's way, as I was to discover.

I had left college and the huge, nondescript building that blights George Square in 1982 and joined a biggish company with a small team of surveyors. My first real boss was John, who, unlike Bill, enjoyed a pint at lunchtime, and sometimes mid-morning too. The door to the room I shared with three others would burst open. 'Right', he would announce, 'let's go over tae Pollok.' I would grab my jacket and off we'd go. He would be wearing his usual attire of heavy sheepskin coat and ironic expression, and he introduced me to the world of Glasgow's construction business. The council were giving out grants to repair tenements and lots of new builders had appeared, often run by 'fly boys', as he called them. 'Remember,' he would say, 'these guys might look like they know it all but they look on you as an intellectual, so don't let them put one over on you.'

With John in the lead, I soon had thirty projects on site and a similar number on the way. Glasgow was self-confident with an air of cheek about it, a condition known as 'gallus' in the local dialect, and gallus was fine with me.

Then the call came to join the National Trust for Scotland.

Bill was a much gentler soul and had been with the Trust for twenty years and we became friends. My father had died a year earlier and, in a way, Bill stepped into the gap. He was part of the panel that was to offer me a role with the Trust in Aberdeenshire as his assistant. He had another in Fife but there was too much activity for them to cope with, and that is where I came in.

When I heard that I was to be offered an interview, I spoke to John and he thought this was a great idea. 'Aye, go for it. You'll soon be an expert.' I laughed, and still do.

Fyvie Castle, cabin ceiling

Pitmedden House

Pitmedden House

It was January when I took the early morning train from Queen Street station in Glasgow to Aberdeen, where I was met by the sparrow-like Jenny, who chirped all the way to Pitmedden, about nineteen miles from the railway station.

I sat in the front of that little car in my new interview suit, knees up at my chin and with my briefcase pushed under the seat, which was rammed forward to accommodate piles of leaflets, postcard and pamphlets. Jenny roared along the country roads and I peered out of the window, waiting for the hills and pine trees I thought Aberdeenshire would contain. My ignorance was both wide and deep and I was nonplussed to be driven by fields and small villages which Jenny would briefly describe before the next rapidly appeared. Finally we arrived, turning left out of the village until the trees lining the roadside verge parted to reveal the small mansion, Pitmedden House, which seemed gigantic to me.

The little car crunched over the gravel in front of the house and Jenny ushered me inside, in a motherly fashion. I was settled into a large, chintz-covered sofa with coffee and a biscuit slightly awkwardly balanced on the arm. Then the fun began.

I was gathered up by Jenny—there can be no other term—for my interview and taken upstairs into the office where five tweed-clad gentlemen waited, who then stood and to my surprise most of them were taller than me. I usually had to look down, being rather tall myself, but now I was looking up. Jenny's husband, Dick, standing on the right of the group, was short and round, the exception to the rule. Trust managers at the time

Bill Hanlin with Maori visitors in Fife

were usually well fed, awfully nice, public school chaps. My old Dad had been a Red Clydesider. He was a factory worker with communist leanings from the period between the wars, and I had arrived from a council housing scheme. How I got the job still baffles me.

Sitting behind a large brown desk, in addition to Bill and Dick, were three factors. Now, that was a job I knew. They collected the rents in the tenements and arranged the insurance cover; my current employers were factors. These, though, were a different type of factor who were more used to gun dogs and the New Town of Edinburgh than the back closes of tenements.

The panel chairman was Donald, whose long face was crowned with a shiny dome and wispy hair. He stuttered a little in his rather old-fashioned received pronunciation. 'I, I hope you had a pleasant journey.' I would come to recognise this pattern of speech among those of Donald's ilk. The repeated 'I' at the start of an elegant sentence is like a tee on the golf course; it sets up the words to be thwacked down the fairway and ensures he has your attention. Donald had been the assistant factor at Candacraig up in Strathdon, and brought from there the joiner I would manage, but that's another story.

I cannot imagine what they saw when I sat before them but they were most definitely a little puzzled. Donald quickly passed the lead to Anthony, the head factor, who had hair like Hugh MacDiarmid and a very direct approach. Mike was the local chap and seemed a bit too big for his own comfort. His large frame struggled to be contained and he bumped the table and peered at me suspiciously. He had a ready laugh, though.

Bill sat quietly, referring to me as 'son' and gently testing my knowledge of slates and stone. I don't recall whether I told him about sand-blasting the tenements, but I took to Bill straight away. This was a common experience for everyone who knew him.

He was a Fifer, living in Crail and working in Pittenweem, where he had led the campaign to save the fisher houses of the East Neuk in the 1960s and 70s. If you visit them today, much of what remains is due to Bill. He saved many of them from demolition and influenced others to do the same.

This came to mind one July morning in 2014 when I received a call while on holiday to tell me of the leak from the

Fyvie Castle, cabin ceiling after the leak

kitchen in the Seton Tower of Fyvie Castle. Calls when off duty are not unusual and there is a sense of responsibility when this happens. This sensitivity had not been natural to me in 1984 when I first came to Fyvie, but it was to develop working beside Bill.

So a day or two later that July, I found myself on the small scaffolding that was helping to protect a ceiling that had been damaged by an overflow of water from a kitchen on the floor above. A tap had been left running and the overflow had failed to do the one simple job it had been designed for.

Standing beside this scaffolding with my younger colleague, as Bill once did with me, I took the opportunity to drone on about how to date decorative plasterwork and how this one might be particularly interesting. It was a Victorian interpretation of a Georgian ceiling and rather delicate, with intertwining ribs and a foliate pattern that swirls around dome-like bosses. Bill would not have droned on, however. He was less verbose and more restrained than me.

I was pleased to note there was no rolling of eyes as I wandered off the point of the visit, which was to decide what to do next. A cruel person might suggest that this is a function of my great age, but I've always done it.

As I made my way out through the Morning Room, which had once been the High Hall of the seventeenth century mansion, I glanced up to admire the interlacing foliage in the ceiling decoration depicting green men with branches flowing from their mouths,

Miss Hunter with Lord Wemyss

and thought back to an earlier meeting in the small room that I had just left. I had stood there with Bill just after we acquired the place, looking at the devastation from a massive leak from the roof two storeys higher. This was just another problem to be fixed in a determined attempt to pull the place into good enough order to open to the public in a couple of years' time.

He said, 'Well, son, that's one for you.' It was the first time Bill had felt able to allow me to lead on some work in the house. This unselfconscious ability to empower others was one of his great strengths, and his son-in-law paid him this tribute in his eulogy. He died in December 2013.

He was stylish in a post-war manner and was always dressed in a tweed jacket with a carefully folded handkerchief, flannel trousers and well-

polished brogues that had a gleam of mahogany. His face reminded me of Fred Astaire, bald with a large chin. He was a man whose interests and charm were shaped by the 1950s, from the hat he wore to the love of Sinatra, and his walk had the gait of Bing or Frank on the golf course.

Before Bill and I got to Fyvie, we worked on other places and with other people. One of those places was Leith Hall, near Huntly, with the folk at the back of Bennachie (pronounced Ben-a-hee and with a peak known as the 'Mither Tap', probably because of its mammary-like profile).

Leith Hall is a courtyard house from the seventeenth century, and Bill and I were to extend the public tour and create holiday accommodation. This followed the death of the tenant, Lady Abercrombie, whom I never met but who intrigued me from the cheeky revision of her name by the Trust curators to 'Lady Apple-crumble'.

They created similar names for others, and at Leith Hall the two elderly sisters who once managed it, Janet and Bunty, are forever known as the Budgies. 'Bunty,' the curators would squawk in faux Morningside accents, remembering earlier visits. 'I think there might be a visitor in the car park. Let's pop down after we finish our tea.' 'Yes, dear.'

Bill would smile, but was too much of a gentleman to indulge in similar innocuous disrespect.

Bill's great gift was to know everyone and usually some of their history. George, the head gardener, whose name in the Doric was Doddie, lived nearby with his wife and aged father, Colin, who would hang from the side of the tractor as it bounced around the grounds, a grin splitting his round, red and shiny face that was unlined despite being well over eighty. That trick stopped when he broke his ankle, falling off when he was eighty-five.

Back over at Fyvie, Bill got to know the ex-army caretaker whom the Trust inherited with the castle. He was used to chasing locals away with the bark of the sergeant of the guards he once was, but soon learned the more welcoming skills expected by the Trust with a little gentle encouragement from Bill.

Colin Stewart at Leith Hall

Later in 1984, in the Seton Tower, he looked over the masonry following the removal of the rotted timber. The rubble, dull grey and unfinished, was visible for the first time since the mason laid it there in the late sixteenth century.

The stones were granite field gatherings placed there by an

unknown craftsman who had worked high above the ground with wobbly timber scaffolding, rope pulleys and wrought iron tools that would have blunted quickly.

In 1984, the building was being prepared for opening the following year and Bill had designed the new tour route through the rooms ending at the great iron yett, a latticed gate of wrought iron bars. The yett at Fyvie Castle is huge and is said to be the Trust's biggest yett yet, guarding the massive door of the Seton Tower. The last room on this route was to be the dilapidated 1960s kitchen where the fittings were removed to make a shop. The last room on the tour in any self-respecting National Trust for Scotland castle is always the shop.

Under the flooring in this room were found remnants of the ancient horse stalls and, looking back, there should have been an archaeologist on the team from the start.

The yett at Fyvie Castle (Jim Henderson)

As Bill stood and looked down at the floor it was clear even to us that this flooring probably dated back to the late sixteenth century.

Bill continued to lead the repairs to Fyvie through into the 1990s until he retired, but before then his office in Pittenweem had been closed and he had to drive each day to Edinburgh, which was not his best time and it made him ill. Every few weeks, as I sat in my office in Pitmedden House, I would look forward to his visit and I knew that the hustle and challenge of the day would be eased by his presence. His arrival would be presaged by the fragrance of the small cigars he enjoyed, and to this day a whiff of cigar smoke evokes for me the effortless quality he could draw from everyone he met.

Bill retired in 1993 and enjoyed twenty years on the golf course, his legacy assured in the places he left behind. At his funeral, I looked around to see I was the only representative of the Trust to attend, his stature and commitment now largely forgotten. I then remembered the wall at Fyvie and the unknown craftsmen and felt that this is just how he wanted it.

3
COMMUNISTS, KILTS AND CONFERENCES

The airport in the Estonian capital was small in 1991, with a wooden shed for customs and passport checks. I queued in the sun with about twenty other travellers and when I got into the shed the guard, wearing a baggy uniform with big red epaulets, asked the strangest security question.

First he asked, 'Do you have any alcohol?'

'Yes, whisky for presents.'

Then, 'Do you have any women's clothes?' This stopped me for a moment.

Yes, he was serious.

'No.'

I did not smile and the barrier was pulled back, the metal rod juddering as it caught on the edge of the plywood kiosk. Later I remembered the kilt, and I wonder what they would have thought of that if they had checked. And why would it bother them? I never found out.

It was late June when I stepped out of the plane onto the tarmac of Tallinn airport in what was then the Soviet Union, at the end of a trying series of flights through several airports. The USSR was not so simple to visit back then, despite Gorbachev and Glasnost. Estonia was looking for a way forward that would draw it closer to Europe and that is why I was there. It was in the throes of a peaceful revolution and conferences were one of the tools being deployed. Peaceful is how it can be described with the benefit of hindsight, but at the time there were tanks poised to roll onto the streets.

At the beginning of the year, tanks had entered Vilnius in Lithuania. Something was stirring in the Baltic states and the Soviet Republic was not too happy about it. As the date for my departure drew near, I remember hearing of Loreta Asanavičiūtė, who had died after she fell under one of those tanks. It was a frightening time and I was to find myself in the middle of it.

The events that would launch me into this revolution began, rather curiously, in York about three years earlier, when I strode purposefully in my kilt through the Royal Hotel seeking the bar, noticing that the wedding band looked bored and the guests were slumped semi-comatose around the ballroom. It was the end of a university summer

Crathes oak door with ancient repair (IMD)

school and I had just left the formal dinner on the campus a mile or two away. My fellow conservators and I thought the place looked a little sad. So I marched up to the stage and asked them if they knew the music for the Gay Gordons, a dance whose name is often misunderstood. It's not about being happy or about sexuality, and its correct title should be not 'Gay' but 'Gey', a Doric word meaning 'very', so the Gey Gordons are the very Gordons, the epitome of Gordonness, just like the army regiment raised in North-East Scotland.

'If you can dance it, we can play it,' the bandleader replied, and we were off. Soon the floor filled and we danced till dawn, or at least till half-past midnight, before heading back to the university for songs and drams.

In those days travelling down to York or London was the only way to hear the latest in good conservation practice, so when I got back to Aberdeenshire I spoke to the boss and decided to have a conservation conference here in the North East. In the tradition of Mickey Rooney we said, 'Let's put on a show,' and we did.

No one knew if anyone would come, so the smallish Great Hall at Crathes Castle was booked. I needed a star attraction and the biggest in the conservation world at the time was John Ashurst, who was the leading authority on the cleaning and repair of historic stonework. The thought of a conference in a castle was too much to resist and he agreed. This attracted others and we had a super line-up. I began to feel like an impresario filling the Glasgow Empire on a Saturday night, hopefully without the reputation that venue had as the graveyard of English comics.

The delegates were fighting for tickets and we could have filled the hall twice. It was April and the sun, the daffodils and the castle worked their magic, and to my great surprise I was asked by the Estonian Heritage Society to travel to the Soviet Union to speak.

'Estonia?' I muttered. 'Where's that?' I had no idea. The Scottish education system had let me down and I rushed off to the library to find out. These were the pre-Google days.

The Ellon library reference section told me Estonia was beside the Baltic Sea and had had a short period of independence between the world wars. It had been once part of Prussia, and was then absorbed by the Soviet Union. The encyclopaedia informed me that it had 60 per cent primeval woodland, and wolves.

As I emerged from that customs shed the following year, the director of the Estonian Heritage Society, Mart Aru, a tall, lean man with leonine grey hair and a beaming grin, stood peering over the heads of the crowd. He wore a blue checked pullover, which he seemed to wear every day. I later realised that this sweater was woven in the colours of the Estonian flag and was a discreet statement of national aspiration. Beside him was a short chap with coarse black curly hair and beard. This was Toomas Tiival from the university, an entomologist, I think.

'Ah, we were trying to guess which would be you,' said Mart. 'The big one, Toomas thought, and he was right. Let's get out of here before they take an interest,' he nodded at the angry-looking young men in uniform with machine guns.

We walked swiftly away and set off in their Lada, with its cracked windscreen, into town, where I was put into a very swanky hotel built a year earlier by the Scandinavian airline company, SAS. I had just figured out how to operate the shower when a call came through. Toomas was waiting for me in the hall.

We climbed back into the Lada and set off heading far to the south to a university hostel deep in the forest beside a lake, where members of the society and chums of Toomas awaited.

Mart Aru (back, third from right) with the author (far right)

His tiny car shot out of the city and its surfaced roads into the country. The roadsides on our three-hour trip were shrouded by thick woodland and every now and then we passed a small settlement of rough modern houses similar to the poorer quality Glasgow council housing schemes of the 1950s.

Occasionally there would be a troop carrier with Soviet soldiers. Looking at the lorry, Toomas would say, 'Tartars' or, 'Cossacks' or something similar. How wonderfully exotic, I thought, naively.

'I believe there are wolves.' I tried to sound well informed.

'Yes, we have six.' Delivered deadpan.

Eventually, we got to the hostel. Vodka was produced and a jolly night was had. The bottles had the sort of cap that once removed could not be replaced, like a beer bottle, so the vodka had to be consumed. I brought out the whisky to a chorus of 'oohs' and 'aahs', Toomas's eyes seemed to widen and the bottle was carefully taken away, for safe keeping, as more vodka was poured.

Toomas was the chairman and founder of the Estonian Whisky Society and my Laphroaig was to be a rare addition to a future meeting of this group. I did not see it again, but I did see photos of it being consumed, when Toomas visited me back home in Scotland some time later.

Next day I awoke, slightly fuzzy, a small Cossack riding across my skull and with that slightly waxy feeling I remembered from my student days. Climbing back into the Lada, we set off to see the most recent work of the Estonian Heritage Society. It was at this point that I became aware of the revolutionary aspect of the experience.

Each settlement would once have had a war memorial, to the Estonians' independence struggle after World War I. The Soviets removed them as unwanted reminders of this and

Soviet army base near Tallinn

buried them. In the early 1990s, they were being rediscovered and rebuilt. Elsewhere, royal statues from the sixteenth century Swedish period were being restored and rough panels describing Soviet atrocities produced and displayed.

The streets of Tallinn were lined with tank traps and the Soviet soldiers were in their barracks, where I for one hoped they would stay. These days, Tallinn is part of the Baltic cruise routes, but then it might have been on the dark side of the moon.

After a while we arrived in Tartu, where I would speak at the university. The cathedral nearby stood in ruins from the bombing of World War II, and enriching the remaining brick walls were beautiful carved faces. Over the years, my experiences abroad and at the conferences I directed came to influence and colour the conservation of the castles I was caring for. I remembered those faces sometime later when one of the speakers at a conference I had organised was the guru of conservation at the time, Sir Bernard Fielden, a kind and gentle man.

Sir Bernard had been the surveyor of the fabric at a number of great English cathedrals, including York Minster where he underpinned the great central tower, before it could collapse, exposing the foundations, which can still be seen today. They are pinned together with huge post-tensioned stainless steel rods, a technique I was to employ years later when the Seton Tower at Fyvie Castle was in danger of collapse.

The Minster has an ongoing tradition of stone repair and replacement, with a workshop where they recreate the wonderful carvings high up on the building. Both the ancient and modern are often grotesque, and shortly after the work to save the great central tower one of the gargoyles was replaced with the face of Sir Bernard, staring at the tower, mouth agape in terror and eyes staring.

Sir Bernard was wonderful for coining memorable phrases. Looking at the ancient door at Crathes, he noticed the bottom third had been replaced in deep historic time. The repair was obvious but in the same material, oak, and had weathered beautifully. 'Not as good as new. Better than new,' he pronounced. Other bon mots arose when he was looking at an advert for uPVC windows that extolled their paint-free virtue. 'Maintenance free means cannot be maintained.'

Conservation was not the only unexpected reminder of home and hearth as I travelled around Estonia. A curious aspect of my experience there was to find Scots in the most

Rebuilt independence war
memorial

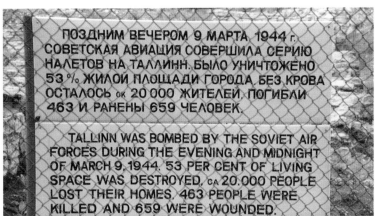

ПОЗДНИМ ВЕЧЕРОМ 9 МАРТА 1944 г.
СОВЕТСКАЯ АВИАЦИЯ СОВЕРШИЛА СЕРИЮ
НАЛЕТОВ НА ТАЛЛИНН. БЫЛО УНИЧТОЖЕНО
53 % ЖИЛОЙ ПЛОЩАДИ ГОРОДА. БЕЗ КРОВА
ОСТАЛОСЬ ок 20 000 ЖИТЕЛЕЙ. ПОГИБЛИ
463 И РАНЕНЫ 659 ЧЕЛОВЕК.

TALLINN WAS BOMBED BY THE SOVIET AIR
FORCES DURING THE EVENING AND MIDNIGHT
OF MARCH 9, 1944. 53 PER CENT OF LIVING
SPACE WAS DESTROYED, ca 20,000 PEOPLE
LOST THEIR HOMES, 463 PEOPLE WERE
KILLED AND 659 WERE WOUNDED.

Discreet subversive signage in Tallinn

surprising places. In Haapsalu, I was guided through the seaside town to its eighteenth century square. The guide stopped and I took my usual place at the back of the group, the better to see both the place and the reactions of my fellow lecturers. He searched the group until his eyes lighted on me, the only Scot there. 'Here,' his eyebrows rose in mock shock, 'once stood the old town wall, destroyed,' a dramatic flourish of hand and arm, 'by Scottish mercenaries in the Livonian wars in the sixteenth century'. I apologised.

Off we went again. The other speakers had arrived and a bus took over from the ageing Lada, bouncing past crumbling gate piers to a nearby mansion. This time the guide was not quite so affable in his discovery of the Scot in his group. 'The last group of foreigners,' he turned away from me, 'included a Scot—the worst communist I have seen.' I thought of my Red Clydesider father.

After these excursions, I was able to wander in the summer evenings to the Lutheran cathedral in Tallinn. I strolled slowly, as one does, peering at the misshapen box pews and dusty memorials. Hanging on the wall over one were flags that seemed to be the Saltire of Scotland in reverse, blue crosses on a white background. This was the tomb of Samuel Greig, a Scottish admiral, and the flags were those of the Russian imperial navy. His Carrera marble memorial was put there by Catherine the Great using material from the winter palace she had been building in St Petersburg. Elsewhere in my travels, I found statues and portraits of General Barclay, who led the Russian troops against Napoleon in 1812. It seemed our greatest export was our soldiers and sailors, with the occasional misguided communist thrown in.

The Estonians were trying to grasp their new freedom during Glasnost. Local beer was produced, flower sellers filled the streets and people were invited to come and support them. There is a photo of me somewhere standing before a big statue of Lenin in a consciously mocking pose. Fortunately, those Soviet soldiers were still in the barracks when it was taken.

Crathes oak door repaired at bottom (IMD)

As my tour of the country came to an end and the conference approached, I made friends with another Heritage Society board member, Kulliki Suurma and her husband Eerik. She was a consultant in the big Tallinn hospital and he was a physicist, and they invited me to their home for dinner.

We took a small bus out of town to the peripheral housing estates. Rows of medium-rise concrete flats blotted the landscape. It had a utilitarian air and was in need of maintenance. We walked up the stairs to their tiny, beautiful flat, shared with three children and grandfather.

I had a wonderful evening. Liivi, their 12-year-old daughter, played Chopin on the upright piano, crammed into one of the two tiny bedrooms. She was amazing and would soon travel to play at the music festival in Aberdeen, and later to work at the Royal Scottish Conservatoire in Glasgow. That evening after dinner I taught them some Scottish dances. Swedish coffee was produced, and eventually I got a taxi back to the SAS, my mind agog.

The conference was in a huge concrete hotel and I was glad to be housed elsewhere. Striding out from that swanky hotel in my kilt, we walked in the sun to the event, causing a bit of a stir. My kilt had the same effect a few years later in Riga, although that conference took place in December and it was bloody freezing.

At the Tallinn conference there were speakers from Finland and other Scandinavian countries. I stood up to read my speech, then looked into the booth at the translator and put the paper down. I could not ignore all I had seen, and I gave an impromptu talk comparing Estonia and Scotland, praising the work of the Estonian Heritage Society in raising awareness of the value of heritage, then sitting down to a bemused look from the translator.

I feared that deviation from my text might have scuppered my relationship with the hosts, but I was invited back a couple of years later to do a lecture tour, and was amazed at how much the place had changed in that short time. Many of the roads had been surfaced, all of the tank traps were gone and the Heritage Society had achieved a well-deserved place in civic society.

After that first conference ended, I took the midnight train on midsummer evening from Tallinn to Leningrad. The white night was lit by bonfires, and I shared the small carriage with two lady Estonian engineers. More vodka was consumed, and when we arrived in Leningrad I was unexpectedly met by a soldier and an Intourist guide. I was not aware my presence was known to the Soviet authorities. They offered me a lift in their big black car but I refused and set off with the two ladies by taxi into town where I was safely deposited at my hotel. The ladies disappeared, never to be seen by me again.

A few days later, I flew out to East Berlin, just after the wall came down. The Aeroflot plane was a bit like a 1950s bus, with overhead netting for the baggage, and the inflight meal was black bread, herring and thin yogurt to drink.

In Berlin, I was able to walk up Berliner Strasse, passing the Victory monument to the Franco-Prussian war, heading to the Brandenburg Gate. Memories of an exam room and history papers came unbidden to mind, bringing a cold sweat.

The author with Lenin

It was a long, long walk in the summer sun. Getting nearer, I was a little disappointed to see the scaffolding up and the gate closed. Now, I like scaffolding, as any surveyor would, but I had hoped to walk through, so I went round into East Berlin and sat on the steps of the Reichstag with its burned-out dome. What, I wondered would my dad, who was in the RAF during the war, have thought of this?

I have retained many friends from those days. Toomas, for example, became a diplomat in the early days of independence. Estonia at first had no diplomatic service, so Britain stepped in to provide some training. Still, the diplomats were few, so they divided the world into three parts with three new ambassadors covering the East, the West and the Rest.

Toomas got the Rest and his first diplomatic guest was from Saudi Arabia. He related to me how he was waiting for the limousine to arrive, not knowing what to expect. Standing there in his new, slightly ill-fitting suit he saw a large black car with smoked windows and he welcomed the sheikh in his full flowing white robes. At that point he knew they were free.

4

WEEPING STONES AND
AN UNPREDICTABLE BULGE

Fyvie Castle was about to open and I was in the crowd along with all those responsible for acquiring and repairing the castle and for developing the tour, when I saw the BBC cameras with the old laird. I wondered what he was saying. 'Do you,' asked the man from the Beeb, 'expect the Trust will build a tower too?' The Castle has five towers, called Preston, Meldrum, Seton, Gordon and Leith, named for the five families that have owned the place since the thirteenth century. Some say, erroneously, that each family built a tower.

'No,' said the old laird. 'They'll probably build a toilet block.'

Sir Andrew was the last resident laird and the castle could no longer be inherited by a member of the family, confirming the ancient curse that said oldest sons would not inherit. A strange truth is that this has often been the case. Death, misfortune and girl children have helped maintain the myth.

The curse was laid by Thomas the Rhymer, the thirteenth century prophet who appears in medieval stories and who, it is said, was taken away by the Queen of Elfland and gained the gift of the second sight. In some parts he is seen as a beneficent character, but not in Buchan. The story says that he would visit one day and would expect the door to be open for him in joyful anticipation. Years rolled by and he never came, until the door was finally closed and there he was, standing at the closed door and not at all pleased. He made his dire announcement and told of three 'weeping' stones that would have to be found and removed before the curse could be lifted.

> Fyvie thou'se never thrive,
> Lang's there's in thee stanes three:
> There's ane intill the highest tower,
> There's ane intill the ladye's bower,
> There's ane aneath the water-yett,
> And thir three stanes ye'se never get.[2]

General William Gordon by Pompeo Batoni (1708 -1787)

Fyvie Castle by James Giles RSA (1801-1870)

The stone in the 'ladye's bower' is a well-known treasure of Fyvie and a phenomenon that would be displayed from time to time, saturated with moisture even on the driest days.

I was the last person to see the stone weep.

In 1984, I arrived to begin the process that would see the house open to view, and Alex the caretaker emerged from the back door to welcome me. Alex had been an army staff sergeant and retained a bristling moustache. He reminded me of PC Murdoch from the Oor Wullie cartoon strip in the *Sunday Post* of my childhood, a newspaper that could be found in every Scottish home in the 1960s. The old saying was that Scotland would never be free till the last Kirk minister was strangled by the last copy of this illustrious publication, famed for its couthy advice, conservative disdain and stories of wee kittens stuck up trees.

Alex produced tea and biscuits and then I was sent off alone around the rooms with their shutters closed and curtains drawn. My feet clacked along the ground floor corridor in the dim light of 60W bulbs. Climbing a narrow stair, I pushed on a heavy, stiff door, so I put my shoulder to it and realised it was steel, painted to imitate wood. It creaked back to reveal the Charter room. The high vaulted ceiling was decorated with a few small armorial panels in the plaster and the walls were covered by dark oak panels enriched with carved figurative decoration. Opposite the entrance was a corner cupboard with a bowed door. I opened it and there on a shelf was an earthenware bowl, inside which was a smaller, broken bowl and in this was the weeping stone.

It was saturated and its surface glistened in the dull light from the barred windows. Unthinking, I reached out to touch the damp and my finger sunk slightly into the surface. I had forgotten an unbreakable rule with collections: don't touch. But, I reasoned, this was a stone and I am a surveyor.

'Oops,' I thought. I closed the door and moved on. Later, I returned with the curators and found the stone dry. It has never been wet again. It was moved out of the cupboard onto a table under a window and covered with a perspex box.

Fyvie Castle Charter room

I fear its weeping days are over. Who can say whether this was due to my touch, the passing of the castle out of private hands or being slowly baked in the sun in its own little glasshouse?

As the team set out to prepare the castle, our approach in the 1980s was not what it would have been just a few years later. The team, of which I was the most junior member, knew that this was to be a great opportunity to save the place and its contents,

The weeping stone

but the decision to get it repaired and open in 1986, only two years later, was an unforgiving timescale.

'Let's all gather in the Noddy House,' the posh curator suggested for our meetings. I was puzzled and replied in Scots, 'Ye mean that totie wee hoose over to the side?' pointing to the small building next to the main castle. Flummoxed, the curator nodded.

Soon we sat shivering in a tiny room on the first floor and plotted the way forward. An architect was needed and

John Batty and Christopher Hartley, the curators

a local one was chosen. Old Sandy, as I called him, was based in the market town of Inverurie, though he was originally from the even smaller town of Insch a few miles away and referred to himself as an Inschite.

He could usually be found in a small, first-floor office over the clacking machinery of an old print works and would move sedately, small cigar in hand, in his immaculate grey Volvo to and from the castle, which became his great love. Despite his country architect demeanour, Sandy had worked on a number of historic places, especially in Monymusk where he was involved with the big hoose and the Norman tower on the local kirk.

I walked through the place with Sandy and Bill, the old surveyor, trying to decide what to do. Standing on the lawn, we looked at the old cement harl peeling away in large brittle sheets, letting water pour in, rotting the timber. Even an inexperienced eye could see that the wiring was antiquated and an imminent fire risk. In one corner, a rattling lift was run from an ancient motor on the roof. I hauled the gate back and climbed in and it would creak and groan and judder to the top.

Sandy soon had scaffolding on the great south elevation, the masons hammered away and the rubble walls began to emerge. The masons were from Inverurie, where an old family firm had slated roofs and harled walls for decades. The squad would arrive in trucks and vans, rolling out with ancient tool bags, tackety beets—work boots with metal studs or 'tacks'—and, if pressed, hard hats.

Wullie the foreman was a taciturn Aberdonian giant, labouring through wind, sun, snow and sleet. He was always there. It was Wullie who rediscovered one of Fyvie's hidden treasures while tapping away at the cement. He was in the middle of the elevation on the wall under the massive arch linking the two drum towers of the great south facade, where he found tightly jointed red sandstone, rather than the usual rubble walling.

Wullie called on Sandy and they peered at the wall. The masonry was deep red with very tight joints and, smoking pipe in hand, Sandy knew to stop. Very carefully the cement was peeled away. Careful not to lose the delicate stone surface, Wullie slowly revealed a huge panel of red ashlar from the late sixteenth century that had been sheltered from above by the great arch. This architectural statement is still visible thanks to Wullie.

When the harl was carefully removed from all of the main walls we realised that the deep red stones that formed the window edges should have been visible, like that panel, but had been covered in the 1960s. The carefully cut stones should have framed each window in the mass of the rough harl, but many were now beyond repair and had to be replaced.

The walls elsewhere are built from random rubble, mostly field gatherings left there by retreating glaciers, rather than quarried stone. These boulders would have been picked up and carted back to the site by those forgotten craftsmen who worked on them with a big

The Seton Tower at Fyvie Castle (Jim Henderson)

hammer to knock them into shape. I stood on the scaffolding with the mason to ask if they had ever done this. 'Och aye,' says Davie in a sing-song Fife accent, 'but ye just have to be sure it's no like a cow's heid when you're finished.'

I learned that these window margins are called 'starts', an abbreviation of 'upstart'. This is because the walls are built with unevenly sized boulders and it is not possible to structurally tie them into the main wall. They stand on the end of the window sill and support the lintel above. Starts are all different lengths, probably depending on the size and quality of the block the mason was working with. If they are built into coursed stonework they are called 'rybats' and are usually the same dimension.

One wet day, a troublesome individual with a degree of authority was looking at the works and saw the new starts. He called to Davie, complaining that the new stones were different lengths. Davie, cheerful and feisty as usual, put the cigarette he was smoking into the mouth of a wee stone man decorating the top of a turret and carefully explained starts and rybats, noting that the individual perhaps didn't know what an upstart was!

Davie the mason

As Sandy, Bill and I set off on this journey we gathered around us those with knowledge, including our colleagues in Historic Scotland. John Knight, the architect and a wonderful artist, and Richard Fawcett the inspector were two of the most experienced and expert people in Scotland. Richard went on to be the Chief Inspector of Historic Buildings for Scotland. We stared at old photographs from the 1960s that clearly showed some interesting cracks on the west drum of the Seton Tower. We would make haste slowly there.

One summer's day in 1985 as the harl was removed we uncovered the cracks and found that the tower was wrapped with iron bands, deeply embedded in the wall. They stretched through the castle to the back wall and on closer inspection we found that these were railway rails. Railway rails?

Lord Leith, in the late nineteenth century, seemed to have an interesting relationship with the railway. He was a steel millionaire from America, which along with the peerage probably gave him a little clout with the railway company. So much so that Fyvie station is not in the village, but was built several miles along the road near the gate to the castle, where each week his staff gathered the laundry from his London home in great wicker baskets, to wash in the soft Scottish water before sending it back south. I sometimes wonder what the local folk thought of this as they tramped up the road to catch a train in the soft Scottish water falling from the sky.

These rails caused us a difficulty. Iron rusts and then expands. There was a possibility that this would in time damage the building. After a long deliberation, the rails were

removed and the tower was strengthened with grouting and concrete in a massive engineering challenge.

Over the next five years each side of the castle was repaired, culminating with the newest, the Leith Tower, and in 1990 the major repairs were complete. The castle looked lovely, a little over-restored from this viewpoint, twenty years or so later, but applauded at the time.

Then a hairline crack appeared on the Seton Tower. Then another one began nearby. Sandy and I stood on the lawn from time to time, peering as this fine line extended up the buildings slowly but with unyielding momentum. Sandy and I kept an eye on this, and a couple of years later we worked on the first holistic condition survey and agreed that this had to be investigated. Not long after this, Sandy, to everyone's shock, died. He is much missed.

I monitored the cracks as they grew in length and width. I remembered the conservation guru Sir Bernard Fielden telling me not to worry about a crack till I could put my fist into it. However, I could see that this crack was active and dynamic. I could not wait for the fist test.

Soon I was working with a remarkable engineer, John Addison. John is a pragmatic, tactile engineer, never afraid to get his hands dirty, unlike the pinstripe-suited chartered engineers I had been used to. He liked to get up close to the problems he was asked to resolve and he approached these issues with a practical intellect, grounded in conservation philosophy. He remains today Scotland's premier conservation engineer.

John was a regular at my Trust conservation conferences in Aberdeenshire. At one event in the mid 1990s, I introduced the problem at Fyvie. I described the rubble tower with its old railway rails as 'a bag of tatties tied around the middle with string'. 'No,' he challenged me. 'It's a bunch of daffodils tied with string.' I was considering the masonry as loosely held lumps of stone with the ability to move around. He was referring to the vertical forces pushing down, inadequately held by the bands. He was more right than I was, of course.

Well, we got to look at the Tower and we both became more worried. An analysis of the ground confirmed there was no settlement problem and a review of the structure and its development revealed that the problem had arisen from the introduction of new fireplaces

John Addison

in the eighteenth century, by the Gordon family. They put in flues by coring through the walls. Unfortunately, the walls in the drum tower are too thin to cope with this disruption and it looks as if there may have been a collapse in the tower at the time of these changes. You can see a rebuilt area in the small room at the bottom of the tower.

Elsewhere in the castle, up in the drawing doom at the top of the Gordon Tower, there is an amazing swagger portrait of Colonel William Gordon of Fyvie standing among the ruins of Rome. He put the fireplaces in and caused the problem. I began to fear that Rome would not be the only place in ruins.

The cracks on the tower are vertical and frame a bulge. It seems that in removing the old bands and introducing grout, this bulge had begun to move again and was now unpredictable. That is to say it might have stabilised and not been a risk or there could have been a sudden catastrophic collapse.

This was the late 1990s, ten years after the first cracks reappeared, and we had to move quickly. John Addison designed a temporary solution and an urgent meeting was held with the new Historic Scotland architect. The local authority granted temporary listed building consent.

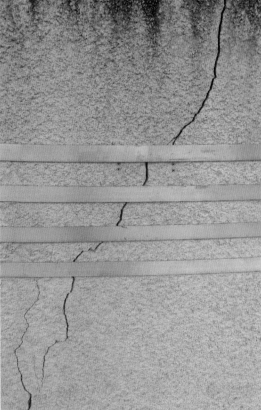

Stainless steel bands on the Seton Tower

34

Crown on the Seton Tower with the Scottish lion,
perhaps with a relocated head
(Graciela Ainsworth Conservation)

The armorial achievement of Alexander Seton
on a dormer window at Fyvie
(Graciela Ainsworth Conservation)

The elegant solution was to wrap post-tensioned stainless steel bands around the exterior of the tower and tie them into the main wall of the castle. They are in a distinct pattern that, I discovered later, mimics the strings of a mandolin, the musical instrument that John Addison plays. The bands worked, the unpredictable bulge is fully restrained and we have monitored the tower ever since.

Some people do not care for these bands and see them as an eyesore. Others appreciate the minimalist aesthetic of the modern materials and see this as a worthy development in the history of the castle. Most, I think, pay them no attention. In 2014, the *Press and Journal* newspaper in Aberdeen described them as 'beautiful'.

5
GHOSTS

Do you believe in ghosts?

In 1983 I lived alone in the North Wing of Haddo House, known as Dawson's flat, from the name of an occupant in days gone by. I had little furniture and existed in the corner of one large room. Most nights as I settled into my bed, just as my head hit the pillow a screech would split the air from outside the window over my head. A bird, perhaps. But why just as I settled for the night? Some people, it seems, are a lightning rod for odd experiences, and supporters of the Trust can be particularly susceptible.

Light at the flick of a switch had already chased many of these beliefs into a place where a frisson of the supernatural was a pleasure. The incidents and tales that follow are perhaps a faint echo of the time when deep shadows filled the corners of our homes and science had not yet banished the spirit world from our health and home.

Throughout the county are Women's Rural Institutes or Women's Guilds. Each one has a social convenor and they all need to fill the winter with interesting events for their members. This means that there is a steady trickle of requests to give talks about the Trust.

As I am known to be fond of the sound of my own voice, I often receive these requests and one, many years ago, was to Fogieloan, deep in rural Aberdeenshire.

Fogie is actually called Aberchirder, but everyone calls it Fogie.

Now, Fogie is about as rural as you get and in winter it is silent and windswept. On those nights the folk are either at the Rural or the pub or the telly. The yellow from the streetlights barely penetrates the mist and drizzle.

I arrived one February night in 1990 in the dark, trying to find the church hall. There was no one to be seen and I drove slowly up and down the few streets between the plain granite terraced houses. Eventually I spotted a light behind one, and found the church.

The Guild ladies were very welcoming as I put up the screen and set up the carousel projector. The convenor approached. She was douce, perjink and clearly in charge. I suspect she was the Kirk beadle too. There was a bustle of activity and just before the meeting was opened with a short prayer I was asked, 'Would you mind judging the cakes at the end of the evening?'

Daisy wheels, Marian marks and 'fire insurance' burns (Jim Henderson)

'Oh yes,' I thought. 'I am qualified as a Trust speaker now.'

My talk was met with quiet indifference. I could not raise either a chuckle or an eyebrow and eventually I took questions. Rather, I took no questions until I mentioned ghosts. The ladies took an interest and a lively debate followed, which took me up to the cake competition. I chose the chocolate one for no other reason than that I like chocolate cake. There was a happy face in the audience and a few scowls, and the evening ended after I packed my stuff away and escaped, covered in crumbs.

I do not believe in ghosts, really. Despite the strange events I told to the ladies of the Fogie Church Guild, these stories have over the years been added to with the experiences of friends and colleagues—people who are unlikely to exaggerate or create fantasies.

When, in 1983, I travelled to that large room in Dawson's flat in Haddo House to take up my new job as assistant surveyor in the Trust's Grampian region, I left my poor old mother white-faced and peering sadly out of the window in the tenement where I grew up, and drove away in a small van, hired especially for the occasion to carry my furniture. I was met at Haddo by the tall, stooped figure of the local factor. He opened the door to the apartment next to the chapel on the ground floor of the north wing. The few items in the van did not take long to carry into this flat—just a bed, a chair and a portable black and white TV.

Haddo House, north pavilion chapel entrance

Ian Gow

Haddo House is about twenty miles north of Aberdeen and the closest town is Ellon, about six miles away. Ellon is a dormitory for Aberdeen and not much happens there. As a result I was usually on my own in the mansion, apart from old Lady Aberdeen, who was about 100 metres away in the south wing, safe behind security alarms and locked doors.

Haddo, like most Trust properties, is a visitor attraction and in the summer is open to view, but its relative remoteness means that it is not hugely popular and the small trickle of visitors did not require a lot of staff to service them. In the evenings I would have the place to myself and would sit in the rose garden to read and soak up the sun. At night, when the house was closed and everyone had gone, the doors would be locked and the security alarm activated.

I would then be alone in the north wing, where my flat covered most of the ground floor. Above me was an old bedroom that had been converted into a catering kitchen furnished with stainless steel and washable surfaces and next to this was the library, carpeted with the biggest chenille carpet in the world, as I was informed by the chief curator, the delightful, wistful Ian Gow.

Most nights when everyone had gone and I was in my room I would hear the door to the catering kitchen above me open. Footsteps would track diagonally across the vinyl-covered floor and I could hear muffled voices. I knew I was the only person there and that there could be no one upstairs. As I looked up at the ceiling I would think to myself that maybe someone had sneaked through from the south wing, but I realised this was unlikely, even if on occasion there had been someone there. The sounds could be heard almost every night. My ears would strain to make out what was being said, in what was apparently a one-sided conversation, but I could never make any sense of the sounds. Each time the muttering would continue, intermittently, for a few hours and eventually I would fall asleep.

I shared this experience with people and was told by Mrs Stanger, the long-suffering cleaner and guide, who had served old Lady Aberdeen for decades before the Trust took up custodianship, that the most likely explanation was that this was Archie, the ghost of Lord Archibald Gordon, who died in 1909—curiously, one of the first people in Britain to be killed in a car accident. He seemed a rather disinterested intruder and we left each other alone.

Everyone at Haddo was less worried about old Archie than about the wiring. The old electric cables were a fire risk and as I looked around I found that their vulcanised India rubber insulation was so brittle it snapped if touched, exposing the bare copper wire.

Two Little Home Rulers, Dudley Gladstone Gordon and the Hon Archie Gordon 1890,
by Louisa Starr (1845-1909)

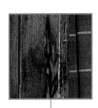

Haddo would be occupied from time to time by guests of the quietly charming Marchioness, who together with her late husband had formed a musical society in the 1940s and was a well-known conductor. Elderly, genteel ladies from the large farmhouses nearby sang with abandon in her choir and would tell me that it had been a lifeline in a cultural desert. They remembered that in the 1960s musical luminaries would visit and stay. Sometimes I would pluck up the courage to intrude on the office of the terrifying and aloof choral secretary, down a dark corridor on the ground floor. Her room was piled high with ancient manuscripts and ragged programmes threatening to topple on to her as she sat at a minuscule desk. On the walls, where they could be seen, were yellowing posters of long-forgotten concerts and I pointed to the one with the brooding Russian pianist Sviatoslav Richter. She sniffed, 'He was very rude.' I could find out no more.

I always trod warily as I toured the place, especially in the bedrooms, where it was not unusual to find them being prepared for these artistic visits, heated by ancient electric radiators, propped on armchairs or set beside dusty tasselled bedspreads.

I rewired the place between 1985 and 1987 and we got rid of the lethal heaters. The electricians arrived from the local town and we dealt with those bedrooms before moving into the chapel at the north end, next to my old flat. The electrician became aware one day of someone standing beside him, looking a little lost. The man was dressed in tweed, wearing plus-four trousers, and asked if he knew where Lady Aberdeen was. Lady Aberdeen lived at the other end of the house and the bemused look on the visitor's face encouraged the electrician to offer to guide him through the maze of corridors. They set off until, about halfway there, the electrician turned around to find he was alone so he stomped back to his tool box.

Haddo seemed to be a hot spot for such phenomena and much later a new property manager spoke to me about several odd events. From time to time as he was closing the house, and sometimes when taking a tour through the bedrooms in the centre of the house, he would hear a door to the attic rattle and bang. 'What did you do?' I asked and he would laugh nervously at the memory of the climb up the bare stone stair to the top landing in the centre of the building, where he watched the door shudder. 'Hello,' he called, fumbling for his key. 'Just a minute.' The rattle, he said, continued until he touched the handle, when it stopped. He told me that he gently pushed the door ajar before purposefully striding in, ready to confront the intruder but there was no one there.

My morning routine at Haddo was Spartan. There was no shower, just a chipped basin and stained bath, and no heating. 'Just as well it's summer,' I thought while making my ablutions. Then after a cup of tea I would reverse my ancient Ford Cortina out of the pend, avoiding the wall roses and hedges around the chapel, to drive to my office at Pitmedden House about seven miles away. Before I left I would check that all the doors in the flat were closed, although I knew that when I got back at night they would all be open. Perhaps Archie was the culprit.

Pitmedden House after the fire of 1807

My trips to Pitmedden were uneventful, other than to spot the aged gardener, Homer, puttering in the opposite direction on his scooter. Old Homer always had a smile and chuckle, and despite being only five foot or so tall with a terrible curvature of the spine, he laboured mightily to keep the Haddo gardens blooming.

I had been at Pitmedden for about two years when the main house was occupied by a new property manager, Grace. She had moved up from Preston Mill near Edinburgh. Huge pantechnicons offloaded her belongings and her family departed after a few days. She stayed there alone for a couple of months awaiting her husband, who was about to retire from his job in Edinburgh. She was small and slight with straight bobbed hair, and reminded me a little of a Roald Dahl character. We walked through the house exploring the rooms and I told her about the Haddo noises and she tried to allay my anxiety by suggesting that creaks and squeaks happened in an old house as they heat up or cool down. 'Pitmedden has the most *awful* noises,' she said.

The Pitmedden House that Grace occupied is mostly mid-nineteenth century and built around a much older core with a great arched fireplace of the earlier building in the dining room. This remnant is all that remains visible of the house before a catastrophic fire that left it virtually destroyed in 1807. The ruin was replaced in 1853.

One morning I was in my office and Grace bustled in to speak to me. 'You'll never guess,' she said. 'Last night I was asleep in the small bedroom next to the bathroom and suddenly someone grabbed my ankles.' I looked up. 'Then all of a sudden they started lifting my feet and banging them onto the mattress.' I raised an eyebrow. 'I thought

Alasdair had arrived early.' Two eyebrows now. 'It was too dark to see and when I got the light on it stopped... and the door was open. Someone must have been left there after the fire and was trying to wake me, 170 years too late,' she giggled.

The Trust seems to attract redoubtable ladies. In addition to Grace, over at Castle Fraser we once had a formidable property manager who had been a PE teacher in Rhodesia, as it was then called. Trina lived in the west wing with her wee dog, Bobbie. Her flat was on the first floor and you entered it from a door in the courtyard that took you to a wooden stair winding up to the door to the sitting room.

Trina was unflappable, so when I was over there with the architect who would write the next condition survey, Sandy from Inverurie, I took the opportunity once our business was concluded to tell Trina about the weird phenomena at Haddo and Pitmedden. 'Well,' she said, 'I can top that. In the evening, when I am up in the sitting room, the door to the courtyard will open and footsteps climb the stair. Bobbie jumps up and sniffs the door, but there is never anyone there. Poor wee Bobbie gets all untoward and charges about, tail up, for ages.'

Sandy heard this and added to my store of wakeful nights by telling me that in the evening, if he was in the main body of the castle, he would make his way up the turnpike stair, passing small rooms filled with sixteenth century oak furniture. On his way back down this furniture was often on its side. Sandy did not care for this experience and I tended to find his draughtsman working late in the afternoon more often than him.

With Grace at Pitmedden and Trina at Fraser, they were joined by Steve at Leith Hall, another formidable woman. When I bowled up in 1983 an army couple were managing the house. Lt Col Sandy Le Gassick became the new regional director in 1984 and his wife, Steve, took on the role of property manager. They had travelled the world after World War II and Sandy was in Palestine as Israel took shape. I discovered that he had also been part of the secretive operations at Bletchley Park during the war. Now, one of Steve's missions in life was keeping her Sandy in good trim and she had his diet well managed, but she wondered why he never lost weight. Could there be something mystical involved? I never mentioned his daily trip to the baker next door, but his secret is out now!

In the evening before activating the alarm, Steve would walk around the house carefully closing doors and extinguishing lights. We were sitting at the large kitchen table of her flat in the south wing, mugs of coffee in hand, when she told me that in the north wing, which is the oldest wing, the last bedroom she would enter when closing up at the end of the day was one with two doors, as it led through into the

Lt Col Sandy Le Gassick
(Robert Grant)

43

Family, tenants and staff at Leith Hall

Banff room. She asked, 'Who put the bloody light switch at the other door?' I smiled innocently. 'When I go in I have to turn the light off and walk though in the dark.'

'Did you trip?' I asked.

'You won't believe this,' she said. 'When I get about halfway across, a little girl laughs.'

'What do you do?' I asked.

'Move faster,' she replied.

I suspect that all these tales have a logical explanation. Some may be centuries old. Sometimes the stories are deliberately fabricated, then repeated as if they are truth.

It's only a couple of generations since we here in the North East lived largely in the dark. Each day would be spent outdoors lifting stones from fields or walking to and from our destination. A journey that today takes minutes would then have taken hours and light during the long winter nights would have depended on fire. Our homes would have been draughty and dirty by today's standards.

Precautions against evil were taken in these houses that sometimes related to Christianity, but others were older. The castles of Aberdeenshire quiver with the resonance of these memories and there is tangible evidence awaiting the observant. Cats are still thought to have special relationship with the occult. Curiously, black cats bring luck in Scotland but the opposite elsewhere and they were sometimes buried within houses to protect the inhabitants.

At Crathes Castle it is said that the spirit of a young woman searches for the body of her dead child. This is not an unusual story and is a favourite in many places. At

Crathes, however, it is said that the body of the child was found under the hearth of a fireplace after the great fire that almost destroyed the place in 1966. I knew the surveyor who found a skeleton there, but it was the skeleton of a cat, not a baby, probably deliberately put there to protect the family from the evil eye. It was in the Green Lady's room, where if you read the words on the ceiling it implies this was used by the women of the house, advising them to avoid 'naughtie' company.

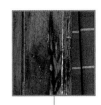

Sometimes the poor cat would be spared and a daisy wheel would be used instead. These are small carvings of circles with the interior divided into petal-like segments. Another carving is called the Marian mark and looks like an elongated M. They are often located where there are draughts of air that might be taken as spirits moving. Sometimes they are also found next to burn marks, which may have been a form of insurance where pre-burning the timber protected it from further burning.

Craigievar Castle stands on its hill where Danzig Willie, the first Forbes laird who acquired an old tower and had it enriched into the iconic castle it is now, and his family have left us a few tantalising reminders of their hopes and fears. Their precautions are still there to protect Craigievar from disaster, whether this is natural or supernatural; the distinction was probably blurred. All three scratches and burns are to be found on the end of the box bed in the housekeeper's room. The bed sits at the door to the stair close to another door and must have been at a crossroads for draughts. I can imagine Willie there in nightshirt and tasselled nightcap watching the curtain ripple and shift in the candlelight.

As the dark was being banished by gas or electric light and the steel baron Lord Leith arrived at Fyvie Castle, an American guest of his stayed in a bedroom off the Dunfermline

The Muses room ceiling at Crathes (IMD)

Bed recess at Craigievar

corridor. Next day he arrived at the breakfast table looking a little untoward, having being awoken by strange noises. When the Trust acquired this castle, one of the curators decided to test this and slept overnight in the same room. He too was awoken by the door opening. It opened its full width and then gently closed. I asked what he then did. 'Pulled the duvet over my head.'

The most famous ghost story at Fyvie concerns the death of Dame Lilias Drummond and the inscription of her name on a window sill. Lilias died in her late twenties in 1601, starved to death by her husband of nine years, Alexander Seton, who went on to marry Lady Leslie only six months later.

In 1984 I met the estate accountant Bob Storey when I was on my first visit. Bob, a quietly spoken, gentle individual who carefully administered the family business for thirty years, took me to see this sill, high up, close to the attics. It was gloomy, so he drew the curtain and opened the shutters.

Bob's appearance was a little like that of Alec Guinness in *Tinker Tailor Soldier Spy* as he gazed at me through large spectacles. 'The laird locked his wife in a small room at the top of the great wheel stair and he left her there till her screams and sighs stopped and she was disposed of,' said Bob, moving closer to the window. 'The laird remarried,' he looked disapproving, 'and their first night was spent in this room.' He paused. 'A tap came from the window,' he said as the back of his fingers grazed the glass, 'but it was ignored. The next morning he found the name of his dead wife carved on the sill, as if by someone floating outside the window'.

You can still see this and the guides point it out to visitors. Everyone loves the grisly details and the children repeat it to their friends. As the castle was repaired a few years later, we removed the harl beside this window and found that the ghostly sill was a carved lintel from some earlier door or window, possibly from the time of a marriage or other important event. It is not an original sill and the carving was there before it was reused. No spooky mason, probably no ghost. However, the guides report that there are often visitors, who, when passing the

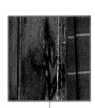

A bedroom off the Dunfermline corridor at Fyvie

murder room, not this bedroom, report a queer feeling. Some have been known to faint, which is not a good idea when you are standing at the top of the great wheel stair.

This intangible heritage seems to be slipping from the castles. The stories are now entertainment, sanitised for the welfare of the young and vulnerable. Custodians of our heritage should take care to capture not only the bones of these beliefs but the flesh and fabric that once made them both real and cautionary tales for our forebears. Conservation should manage the changes needed to help these places survive for future generations, but the danger is that they become mere backdrops for passing entertainment. The myths and legends can tell us so much of long-gone belief systems and perhaps shed a light into that darkening past.

6
FIGHTING BUTTERFLIES

The High Hall of the Old Tower at Drum Castle was a cathedral-like space in 1987 and visitors who struggled up a tight turnpike stair were then faced with a terrifying climb up a long timber staircase to the battlements. When they achieved their goal they could stand with the wind in their hair, but with no explanation of where they were or what they might see, I am sure the experience was something of a loss for most.

David Learmont, the Trust curator, approached me that year with a proposal to create a medieval tableau, complete with raised dais, mannequins and possibly piped music.

David L. was a roguish fellow who, through force of personality, had been at the heart of the Trust for over twenty years and we tended to get on quite well. I liked to baffle him with Scots terminology, asking, 'Is that yon totie wee ane?' of a man whose camp, upper-crust pronunciation turned an electrical conduit into a 'condwee', as if in French. I asked, 'Why are there never any roped-off areas in the properties?'

'You wouldn't expect to visit a friend and find they had roped off the silverware, would you?' he would reply with a twinkle, his eyes peering straight into mine. 'Neither should we. Our visitors are honoured guests and should feel they have the freedom to wander, smell the flowers when a door opens and touch the fruit in the bowls.'

Over the years when he had the chance he would enhance the experience for visitors. Many of the carpets, most of the chintz curtains and loose covers, and nearly all of the kitchen displays were his invention. Despite this approach to accuracy, he wanted a sense of reality and put wine in the decanters and fruit in the fruit bowls. Magazines and newspapers were strewn artfully and wellies placed behind external doors, often with a fishing rod propped nearby. When you get to know the style you can spot his influence everywhere. He was a sort of arbiter of taste and he achieved this with unending charm coupled with unyielding forcefulness, and a conspiratorial wink. Trying to resist his ideas was rather like fighting butterflies. We would disagree from time to time, especially when he wanted to move things around, one example being an old iron hob grate from a bedroom at Leith Hall that he moved over to Drum Castle.

We climbed that tight stone stair in the old tower at Drum to the High Hall, stood on the gritty earth floor and agreed that it was bare and brutal, devoid of human

Drum Castle in the 1850s by Anna Forbes Irvine (1828-1900)

The Old Tower at Drum Castle

comfort and fit only for the most basic medieval existence. The Trust's official position was that the tower was thirteenth century and this was what the visitors were told. However, an investigation has recently placed the tower in the reign of Robert the Bruce during the time when he exerted control in the North East in the 1320s and a sophisticated assemblage of hidden rooms and 'lost' buildings have been found, but that will be another tale.

The Hall was rather like an ancient monument with no glazing, an uneven earth floor and no illumination. The curator strode around that day with great purpose, the shine on his brogues dulling as the dust was kicked into the air. 'What we need,' he instantly determined, 'is a bit of life... it's just so... dull. Let's get some stone flags on the floor and put a raised dais at the end of the room. It will need... mannequins and lutes.' He could see it all so clearly and I stood silently, disapproving. I thought this was going a bit too far without any supporting evidence and soon I appointed a small archaeology team to have a look for something a bit more related to the actual history of the place that we might recreate.

I knew where his enthusiasm might have come from; he had recently installed mannequins at Falkland Palace. They were of a youthful Marquis of Bute and his ageing architect, Robert Lorimer. Lorimer stood there as a grey-haired, balding man enthusing the laird with his grand designs. Lorimer would have been in his early thirties when the meeting was said to have taken place. David L's infectious and enthusiastic relaxed attitude to the facts was further compounded by putting copies of the floor plans of Fyvie Castle in his hands instead of plans of the palace.

I knew one or two archaeologists at the time. With their help, work began and they started to dig up the floor of the old High Hall. Although this was not my first archaeological dig, I was very excited at what we might uncover and was always hanging about looking over shoulders and probably being a complete pain.

'Found anything?' I asked, as the young chap in the trench scraped away with what looked like a teaspoon.

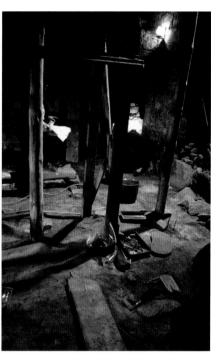

Drum Old Tower archeological excavation

'Yes, we are quite far down now, into the early period, and there has been one find.'

'Oh yes?' I said, containing my curiosity with ill-fitting nonchalance.

'It's a Golden Wonder crisp packet.'

This was the first indoor dig in Trust history. The team found that the High Hall had been divided with a partition wall, which had fallen over and could now be seen buried in the earth floor. It had formed a corridor, called the Screens Passage and there were cobbles where the occupants climbed to the now missing timber floor above.[3]

There had been no stone flags on the floor as our imaginative curator had hoped, but by this time his interest had waned.

There had never been stone flags, nor his raised dais, but there was, to my delight, a rat run through the dirt. Their tunnels worked their way through the earth floor and we found remnants of food bones deep in them, dragged down there from the rushes covering the floor above. A cross-section cut through this floor appeared like a layer cake of alternating brown and white layers. I stood again in the hall asking questions about these layers after they were analysed. 'Well, the brown is faeces,' said the archaeologist, 'and decayed vegetation, and the white seems to be lime powder sprinkled over it to sweeten the smell.' I reminded myself that this was the home of the nobles; goodness knows what it must have been like for the hoi polloi, like me.

David L. decided to do no reinterpretation of the space and never again climbed the stairs.

The Old Tower High Hall at Drum Castle (Jim Henderson)

This was the 1980s and the Trust had only a sketchy understanding of archaeology and what it might be useful for. It was thought of, if thought of at all, as digging holes to find prehistoric treasure.

I am pleased to say that in the 1990s we improved and an archaeologist was employed, but it was not until 2000 that I worked closely with one on the staff, when I was the conservation manager for North East Scotland. Dr Shannon Fraser joined the team and our eyes were opened to the fantastic treasure trove of knowledge that was just waiting to be discovered.

Long before Shannon arrived, in my early years with the Trust, Craigievar Castle was rapidly becoming my favourite place. It had so many interesting problems and I thought this might be like a country doctor meeting a patient with a wide array of exotic disorders.

Geordie the groundsman was worried about the chimney on the top of the old courtyard, or barmkin, wall next to the castle. It was leaning perilously and, he thought, about to fall off. I got Johnnie the joiner over there to put up timber raking shores to keep it up while I thought what to do about it.

Geordie and I stood under the wall. The ivy was huge with thick sections snaking around like a well-fed anaconda. It didn't take long to realise that the wall behind the ivy and below this chimney was being pushed apart and the pointing mortar had washed away.

Soon it was 'fly time' and we sat in his kitchen where his wife had made us tea and scones. He was worried about that chimney because he had to cut the grass nearby and didn't want it to fall on his bunnetted head.

'Well, fit'll you dee aboot it?' he said, leaning back in the kitchen chair, his stockinged feet sticking out, Mrs Geordie having made him leave his boots at the door. I assured him that it would be fixed. Geordie looked sceptical.

The wall sits beside the castle and was probably built in the early sixteenth century but now only this one part remained, held in place with massive stone buttresses that were probably put there to stop it falling over when the other walls were removed.

These things take time, and in 1988 a new property manager arrived. Former Glasgow Police Sergeant David McKay had walked the beat in the streets where I grew up and there was now no hiding place for me. It was as if Oor Wullie had grown up only to find PC Murdoch working beside him. PC David had a cherubic face and was a sweetie with a fondness for bagpipes, fishing and lunch.

He chortled and his expression flitted between puzzled confusion and beaming understanding as he listened to my suggestions. 'Oh, aye, aye, aye,' he said. He loved the ideas I had for the works to the old wall. There would be lime mortar, grouting and maybe a soft top for the wall heads—a method for capping the walls with turf rather than mortar to encourage evaporation—and I had a desire to see the lovely wild flowers return to the wall after it had been repaired. Many years of benign neglect had created a natural rock garden, probably enhanced from time to time by the Forbes-Sempill family.

Earlier that year I had been to see Fountains Abbey in Yorkshire to meet John Ashurst, the great panjandrum of stone conservation at the time. He had the novel approach of repairing ruins so as to leave them apparently in a state of neglect, complete with weeds and wild flowers. As we wandered around the abbey he pointed at a scattering of tourists. 'What do those visitors want from these places? Romance!' he shouted in his Home Counties accent. It should be festooned with cornflowers and creepers. 'Look at that,' he said, staring at a roofless building. It's so hard and bare, without any softening of its edges. 'It's like a boiled sweet.'

Looking at John's ruin that had been repaired many times over the centuries, the small stones in the core of the wall are visible which he described as, 'as if its guts were hanging out'. He and I became friends until his premature death in 2008, and he was a regular speaker at Trust conferences throughout the 1990s.

John was in my thoughts as I was faced with a conundrum at Craigievar, and I proposed something novel. I wanted to use archaeology to guide any repairs and the repair technique was to be new to Scotland, but where, I wondered, was the money coming from? Historic Scotland helped through their architect in the north, who had learned his trade in England and knew of John Ashurst and the new look, and so I was able to secure the funding, though I did have a small embarrassment on the way.

Barmkin wall after repair

Each year I would make my way to Edinburgh, to the Trust headquarters in Charlotte Square, to make my case for the various projects that needed to be delivered. In this case I had confirmation that Historic Scotland would provide some grant funding. I needed the rest of the money from the Trust.

These budget meetings discussed the entire regional budget over a few hours and my project bids were a small part of the process. Around the table would be the director, deputy director, finance director, financial controller, curator and so on. I would sit and wait at the board table—aptly named, I thought, yawning. The room was on the north side of the square with south-facing windows allowing the sun to stream in. The temperature would rise and it could get hot and uncomfortable.

Leaning back on the chair, my eyes drifted to the ceiling. This was an ornate field of foliate patterns and winged figures, all in glorious Technicolor, as David Learmont described it. I slid down in the seat, tilting back for a better view. After a moment or two I heard the director say, sotto voce, to his deputy, Col John Davie MC, 'Ian's asleep'. I didn't move.

'Nope, he's looking at the ceiling.' I waited a few moments and assumed the normal posture, pretending I had not heard.

The following year, after the work was done, the director said at the next meeting, 'I was up at Craigievar, looking at the wall and it looks just the same.' I beamed, and he looked bemused.

On returning north in 1988, ready to begin the repairs to the barmkin wall, I remembered Ian Shepherd, the Grampian Regional Council archaeologist, as I made my way into Aberdeen. Soon I was standing in a huge open-plan space where everyone seemed be hidden behind their own little wall of pot plants and pin boards. Slowly, as if uncoiling from the depths, Ian appeared above the clutter. This tall, bald, bearded man with bottle-bottom glasses spoke with a soft, lisping voice.

We had first met in 1986 at Fyvie Castle, where he tried to find the missing courtyard walls in a tiny excavation opposite the castle door. This keyhole trench was the only bit of archaeology we did at the time and, looking back, that was a huge missed opportunity.

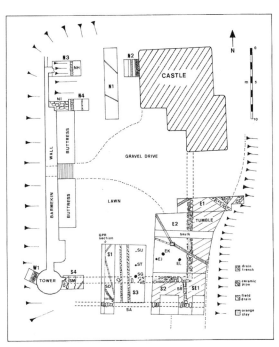

Old Tower 1993 excavation plan (Moira Greig)

Ian Shepherd had an assistant, Moira Greig, who was full of energy and sparkling enthusiasm. She offered her assistance with Craigievar's barmkin wall.[4]

Poor Moira then had the unenviable task of creating a drawing by measuring every stone, just as I had seen down at Fountains Abbey. On a lovely sunny day I arrived to see how it was coming along and Moira had completed the tricky part where the leaning chimney was committed to paper.

'You know that doesn't belong up there,' she said looking up at it.

'Hmmm?' I replied.

'There is no flue. Someone stuck it up there to keep it safe when another bit of the wall, maybe a kitchen, was demolished.'

'Oh,' I said.

'And what's more, it's crushing the wall. The weight and the ivy around it are making the wall bulge out. It's going to fall down one day.'

'Ah,' I said, becoming anxious.

The repairs were to be delivered by a team of masons from St Andrews. They were led by Davie, the mason who had been working on Fyvie Castle. Their boss, Bill Watson, was the owner of the old family firm. He had worked with lime as an apprentice and when I explained what I hoped to achieve he looked at me, tilted his head, sucked his teeth and said in his sing-song Fifer accent, 'Aye, weel, maybe.' Clearly he was sceptical.

Old Tower excavation, Moira Greig on left, looking up

I replied, 'Well, if it was easy, anyone could do it.'

Back in the mid-1980s there was really no one working with lime mortar. Some evangelists had begun to arrive from the south and brave pilgrims were taking the first steps in bringing it back. One or two architects had begun to use it but they tended to be from the hairy, lentil-eating and sandal-wearing fringe of the profession. We needed a John Ashurst to lead us. Historic Scotland knew that lime was the future, started to build their knowledge and helped to create the Scottish Lime Centre in Fife. Pat, the first director of the centre, worked with me a little during a short period when she was their district architect in Aberdeenshire, around the time when we were planning this project.

I really wanted to use local materials at Craigievar and found a source of local sand from an old quarry in a field a few miles away but there were no working quarries for building lime in Scotland and very few in England. I searched around and found some that produced agricultural lime, such as the one at Boyndie Bay on the Moray coast, but the owners could not guarantee its quality for making lime to build with.

So, I turned to England and an old-fashioned supplier from the Totternhoe Lime Stone & Cement Company in Bedfordshire. I knew this firm was used by quite a few conservators so we ordered a batch of quicklime, a highly reactive material that can be turned into lime putty for making mortar. By the time it got to us it had partially slaked in the air and was pretty useless. So Bill travelled down there himself, we eventually we got what we needed and Davie and his mates got stuck in.

They took that chimney down and set it on the ground nearby and it's still there looking like a tiny pulpit for a missing church. Then the ivy was removed and every stone numbered before the wall was dismantled and rebuilt to make it safe, with all the stones back in their original position.

I decided that hidden voids in the wall would be grouted. That means that a liquid mortar is poured in from a watering can, in the hope that it will trickle into the wall and fill up the holes before setting. I had seen this done at Fountains. Little cups made with modelling clay are formed on the walls to act as funnels. I asked Davie where they got the modelling clay. 'Oh, I took it oot the graveyard back hame,' he said. I looked sceptical. 'It has mair body,' he laughed. I never could decide if he was joking.

We got one side of the wall finished before the winter and all of the mortar fell out in the frost. It was too weak; I had made the ratio of sand to lime too big. So next season we redid it and it worked. It was the first successful use of lime mortar by the Trust.

I decided not to try the soft top to the walls. There seemed no need and after the winter frost problem I did not want to take the risk. But I watched the wallflowers return.

As Moira finished her task and while Davie and his mates worked I wondered what Craigievar courtyard looked like before the missing walls were lost. The old wall, now repaired, had a turret at the south end and some people thought that there had been another turret at the missing corner. There is a tendency to view places like Craigievar as if they are unchanged by the centuries, sitting in the landscape like a cup in a saucer. I could not believe that Craigievar had sat there in its parkland for 350 years without leaving evidence of past changes below ground and, inspired by Moira, I became convinced that we needed a bit of research archaeology, so I persuaded the Trust to fund it.

Moira was happy to return, there was a call for volunteers and soon dozens arrived. The dig took place revealing the full extent of the old courtyard. The old wall lay there under the turf in a scatter of boulders. It had simply been pushed over and buried. There was no corner turret.

Now we knew how the castle would have been approached by the Forbes family and their friends. They would have entered this courtyard opposite the only door into the house. The yard would have had some lean-to buildings, perhaps for stabling and storage. Above their heads, the turrets and the projecting stone cannons on the roofline look down. Twenty years later these cannons and turrets were to become something of a challenge for me, but that will be another tale. In the meantime, however, visitors could stand up on the viewing platform at the top of the castle, with the wind in their hair and hopefully a better understanding of the place below. There was no money for fancy interpretation back then, so we simply used the best interpretive tool available: people. The guides, imbued with new knowledge, could weave the tales into the experience offered to visitors.

7

OFFICES, SHOPS AND RAILWAY PREMISES

There was a light drizzle misting the air on my first day with the Trust in April 1983. Backing my car out of the pend next to the chapel at Haddo House near Tarves, I narrowly missed the garden fence before I cruised the five miles or so in my gold Ford Cortina to Pitmedden, where the office was situated over the entrance to the Great Garden, a recreation of the seventeenth century pleasure grounds. I timidly took up my place in a tiny room that had been the bathroom of one of the house's converted flats, and it wasn't long before the door opened.

'Hello, I am Marjory,' was my introduction to one of the secretaries.

'I don't make coffee,' was the second sentence.

'I, I, I neve... I wouldn't... sorry,' I mumbled incoherently as I sat uncomfortably on a post-war utility chair, at my minuscule fifth-hand desk, but I soon discovered that Marjory was lovely, and she was the fastest shorthand writer I had ever seen.

Each morning her American husband Ben would drop her off and she would take up residence at her typewriter, lighting the first cigarette of the day. Dick Hillson, the resident regional director, would arrive later. She looked on with wry amusement, one eyebrow raised, when the director suggested that working for the Trust must be a high point in her career. 'You see,' she would drawl, 'I worked first for Lord Aberdeen way back in the 1950s but soon got away from there and into the diplomatic service.' She tapped the ash into a bowl. 'That's where I met Ben, during the Malayan thing.'

She was referring to the Malayan emergency, as the British government called it, a guerrilla war fought between

Dick Hillson (with red tie) and friends

Ivory, Apes and Peacocks, also known as the Entry of the Queen of Sheba, by John Duncan (1866-1945)

Major James Keith CBE

Commonwealth armed forces and the Malayan National Liberation Army. She would warm to the topic and, after a little encouragement, told me about her time in Kuala Lumpur, when she would take secret night flights in a small pre-war plane across the rainforest with a briefcase of cash ready to pay off someone. I had to wonder if this was Miss Moneypenny with a cocktail and cigarette. Her room was always thick with smoke.

A few doors away from Marjory's smokehouse were the principal rooms once occupied by the last owner, Major Keith, who had run a market garden within the walls and passed the castle on to the Trust in the 1950s.

The small art and furniture collection he left has an eclectic, slightly colonial feel to it and my favourite piece, sadly, was not there. It was on loan to Edinburgh zoo! It is a very colourful rendering of *The Arrival of the Queen of Sheba*, otherwise known as *Ivory, Apes and Peacocks*, one of the symbolist paintings by the great 20th century Scottish painter John Duncan, which Major Keith had bought just after the war. It must have sat uneasily among the other gluepot-style paintings of Hieland coos in the dubs and English cathedrals. Major Keith, it seems, was not totally immune to colour, and he also had a wonderful bright silk Persian rug that can now be seen in Brodie Castle.

I travelled to see the painting, which depicts the queen herself, naked, on top of an elephant, riding through a jungle surrounded by flunkeys and monkeys. I tried unsuccessfully to have it repatriated, and in 2006 when I was the regional director, I asked Ian the curator if it was particularly collectable. 'Oh yes,' he confirmed, looking at the animals, the colour, the jungle and the naked lady. 'It appeals to so many...' he sought the best word, 'interests.'

The Great Garden has two levels and the lower one was transformed in the early days of the Trust to entice visits. This seems to have been a reaction at the time against the grey utility of the post-war years and compromises were made to the authenticity of the design to meet these tastes. Bedding plants were to be used to fill the spaces between the clipped hedges instead of coloured stones, and when the head gardener, George Barron, later to find fame in the BBC's *Beechgrove Garden* programme, was asked about this compromise his reply was, 'Fa'd pay till see a puckle chucky steens?' (Who on earth would pay to look at a few pebbles?)

So it was in 1956 that the cognoscenti gathered around the place and the Chief Inspector of Historic Buildings for Scotland, Dr James Richardson, worked to set the

Highland Cattle on a Moorland, 1895, by Joseph Denovan Adam (1841-1896)

new designs in context. Local architects, Marshall Mackenzie in Aberdeen, removed the porch to the house to create a vista through a new pend into the garden, which immediately became a wind tunnel, freezing Dick Hillson and his wife Jenny, who occupied the adjoining apartment. They could use a cupboard backing onto this pend as a chiller where they could keep ice without a refrigerator for his evening Martini. These were more civilised times.

Dick and Jenny were kind and I was sometimes invited to dinner, where we ate at the widest dining table in the Trust—so wide that if the salt is in the middle you have to climb up on top to get at it.

Dick walked short distances with a busy bustle, but seldom in the garden, and it was said that he would get his car in through the front door if he could. The new garden that George and Dr Richardson created is, in effect, a wonderful example of the early Trust's vivacity; it brims with self-confidence and its colourful display must have dispelled the post-war utilitarian gloom. I now think of it as part of the enthusiastic vibrancy that had brought about the Festival of Britain in the UK and the New Look from Christian Dior in France.

Gardens and gardeners never stand still and they constantly aspire to add interest. So it was in the 1980s when a local farmer, Lindsay Cook, offered a massive farming and domestic folk collection, inherited from his father. All sorts of bric-a-brac was included, ranging from oil lamps to neep hashers—tools for slicing turnips destined

Pitmedden farmhouse, home of the Cook collection

for animal feed, though neeps are something of a delicacy in the North East—as well as tractors and a threshing mill. There was even a bench from a cottar hoose, or farmhouse, whose seat would lift to reveal a metal-lined trough. Here a week's worth of porridge was kept, a slice taken off it each day for the ploughman's lunch.

All this was to become the Museum of Farming Life.

Lindsay was bald, short and perpetually smiling, with a big personality and great business acumen. He walked with the rolling gait that many Aberdeenshire farmers seem to have; I suspect it comes from striding over ploughed fields.

Within a short while of arriving in 1983, I was active with the museum, helping create spaces to display Lindsay's stuff. One of these spaces was in an old farm building with a room that would have once been the bothy, where an itinerant farm labourer would have lived for the duration of his fee.

Feein was a rather unpleasant form of job market before the Second World War, when farm labourers would offer themselves for short-term contracts, often paid at the end of the period, with dinner, bed and breakfast included. Many of the North East's massive collection of folk ballads derive from this time, such as 'Bogie's Bonnie Belle':

Lord Wemyss, Tam Reid and Mike Mackie, Lord Lieutenant of Aberdeenshire

At market day in Huntley toon, twas there I did agree,
Wi Bogieside, the fairmer, a sax-month for tae fee.
Noo Bogie wis a surly carle, and I did know this well
But Bogie had a dochter braw, and her name it was Belle.

I learned this from Tam Reid, 'the Bothy Ballad King', who won the title at an event that attracted an audience of 10,000. He would come along to Trust events at Pitmedden, dressed in a stage version of the pre-war farmer's clothes, nicky tams, tackety boots and bunnet, set off with a bright red neckerchief. Tam and his chums sang to a large and appreciative fan base of brosie locals.

The Cook collection gave us the opportunity to furnish the bothy. An ancient bicycle was parked at the door with Tam Reid singing inside from a hidden speaker over the box bed, where an open-mouthed mannequin lay under the covers. The bike stayed there until a slightly flushed middle-aged lady pointed out that there was a ladies' bike outside the bothy and that this was not what was expected from the National Trust for Scotland. It was removed.

Opposite the bothy was space for a new building. This was to be an open-fronted shed, where the outdoor equipment could be stored and displayed.

One day in 1986, the phone rang and a builder in Aboyne spoke. 'Ye dinna ken me, but I have bought Aboyne Railway Station, would ye like the cast iron columns before the canopy falls doon?'

'Oh aye,' I said and dashed over and negotiated to have them taken down and delivered for free to Pitmedden, where they would support the roof of the open shed.

Ian the gardener, Lewis the mason and I stood and looked at the pile of cast iron when it arrived. The Trust mason said, 'Ye'll need an awful pile of steens.' I wandered back up to the old converted bathroom, wondering where I should source them.

Then another builder called me. 'I hear you're needing some steens.' A nineteenth century derelict cottage about thirty miles away was to be demolished to allow a new house to be built and the owner offered us the masonry. The builder agreed to get the stone and deliver it. That was Tondy from Tarves, a lovely man with tousled, jet-black hair and ruddy complexion whose real name was John Davidson, but as a child John D. morphed into Tondy. He was part of a small dynasty of local tradesmen and had been the last miller at Nethermill, near the village. He would glance up, being rather short, eyeing me with a mischievous twinkle, knowing just what an orra loon I was.

In those days I managed a small direct labour team, which consisted of one joiner and one mason. Lewis, the mason, was a wee bit bullish and would drive his van with frustrating slowness, but he took on the task of building the walls with his usual confident swagger. He surprised me with superb stone cutting when I asked for the date to be carved into the top of the wall. I had some rather trying experiences as I attempted to manage him, but he was a very talented man, cursed with demons that perhaps stopped him from using all the skills he clearly had.

Given my inexperience as a manager, I was fortunate to have the support of the head gardener at Pitmedden. Ian Ross was jolly, with an ancient, battered deerstalker cap pulled firmly onto his balding head. He was at heart a frustrated landscape gardener. There was nothing he liked better than getting a big mechanical digger onto the property.

At weekends Ian could be found strapped behind the huge drum with the local pipe band and at other times with his chickens. He would approach their woodland enclosure with some hesitancy because the cockerel did not like him. The gate would swish over the fallen leaves and when the feisty wee bird became aware that he had entered its domain it would bristle and rush at him. Ian would take off his cap and as the bird jumped, lifting its spurs to try to rake him, he would gently swat it with the cap, *whap*! It would tumble back in a flurry of feathers, gather itself and launch another charge and Ian would scamper out of the way.

Below my old bathroom office in the big house there was a shop and a rather

Ian Ross and friend

64

underused tearoom next door. One day, Ian's wife Alice, as jolly as her auld man, told me with a faint hint of exasperation that there always seemed to be coffee powder at the wall cupboard on the floor in the tea room, but there was no coffee stored there. She was the cleaner and was a bit fed up having to clean this each day. So off I went to have a look and found that the powder was fungus spores and the whole floor, whose timbers sat directly on the earth below, was decayed.

In my youthful inexperience I decided that it all had to be replaced and this was a job for the squad. Johnnie the joiner was as usual quietly content at the prospect. He had arrived decades earlier, having been the estate joiner at Candacraig in Strathdon, many miles inland. There he had worked with his father and after a little questioning from me, he would pause in his gentle whistling to recall the fierce winter of 1946-47. The snow lay deep in the Strath, up to the height of the fence posts, for months and there could be no transport or supplies to the more remote parts. Sheep and the frail died. One job that winter, he told me, was to make a coffin for a small child who had frozen and the memory still haunted him over forty years later.

Johnnie was never annoyed or urgent, even when he cut his finger off in the band saw and that day was seen to stride with his usual slow purposeful walk to get assistance, but before going to hospital he wanted to collect the finger, so we looked in the wood chip and mouse droppings on the floor of his small workshop but it was nowhere to be found. I sometimes wonder if one day it will be discovered and I await the shrieks and the investigations. We got Johnnie some new machinery and moved him to a purpose-built workshop, where he worked on until his retirement in 1992, when we had a big party and he would sing to us in a sonorous baritone, all his tunes delivered at the unhurried and determined pace at which he walked through his life.

Lewis was less keen to help with the floor and he grumbled and moaned, looking at me with vicious sideways glances or dismissive snorts, but at twenty-three I did not have the gravitas to deal with this. Ian the gardener came to the rescue after a few beers in the local hostelry and, taking him to one side, quietly persuaded Lewis to cooperate. The work went ahead as planned and it still seems to be safe and dry thirty years later, but Lewis never really forgave me. He sometimes picked the wrong person to annoy and that included the young gardener, Duncan, who cut the firewood. In those days staff would get firewood in the winter; not so now. Duncan knew the size of Lewis's fireplace and cut his logs a couple of inches too big. Duncan kept his distance when wee Lewis sought him out later, his face fierce and fists clenched.

The happy team stayed in that office over the shop until 1986 before a relocation to Inverurie.

Through that time I often made the coffee for Marjory.

8

BASIL, THE BENS AND THE SPHINX

Travelling north from Perth, long before I joined the Trust, I stopped in a car park just beyond Dunkeld. In the drizzle I got out to stretch my legs under pine trees above a ravine. After walking for a few minutes, I spotted a little building at the end of the muddy path. I wandered in and saw that the end wall was a big opening and the place was filled with the roar of a waterfall. My feet skittered on the muddy floor and my hand grasped the rotting panelling on the decaying walls. I slithered out on to a small balcony and felt the cold spray on my face as my glasses slowly misted over.

Many years later I walked along that path again in the company of Ben Notley, the Trust's property manager for the Hermitage, once part of the most important eighteenth century picturesque landscape in Scotland, with spectacularly large Douglas firs and the amazing folly, Ossian's Hall, overlooking the Black Linn waterfall. Ben and I had been thrown together in a new regional structure and I was the conservation manager. Ben had done amazing things since he arrived twenty or so years earlier but the little building needed some help. The mud was still on the floor and the panelling, though repaired, was looking very sad. As we chatted I learned that Basil Spence, the modernist Scottish architect, had designed the balcony in the 1950s to rescue the building from dereliction, so we galvanised ourselves to wage a long battle to fund another rescue.

In 2000 I was new to working in central Scotland but I knew that, not far from Dunkeld, Spence had designed a delightful home, known as Gribloch, in Stirlingshire. In 1998 the Trust's Council met at Haddo House to consider acquiring Gribloch, but it was not to be. The Trust had taken on the enormous Mar Lodge Estate a few years earlier and was a little reticent about anything new.

I was at Haddo for that debate to give a talk on local Aberdeenshire issues and listened to the discussion but I do not recall any mention of that other Basil Spence design, up near Dunkeld. The Council was a rather bloated decision-making forum where representatives of august institutions sat alongside a self-perpetuating oligarchy, as I once heard it described. It seemed to me that old battles were still being fought by those who thought Mar Lodge had been a risk too far and who now dug their heels in. 'This far and no further.' No more new properties.

Ossian Singing (Calum Colvin)

Ossian's Hall with Spence's work completed

The reticence about new acquisition became part of the culture and has been a feature of the Trust over the past twenty years. I too became affected by this attitude around 1999, when I led the appraisal of Cairness House near Fraserburgh as a potential new property.

For my first visit to Cairness I travelled up to the Broch, as Fraserburgh is known to the locals, stuffed into a single car with a few others on a dreich February day. Fraserburgh is a tough, granite town that sits on the rocky coast and smells of fish, but Cairness is a little way out and can be a challenge to find. We travelled there for an initial reconnaissance and no one was quite sure how to find it, so there was some curious peering over hedges after driving along small farm tracks through the mud and rutted puddles. Eventually we came to a gateway flanked by sphinxes, which were so incongruous that it had to be the estate, and we drove in.

Cairness has a stark elegance that is precise and classically formal. Its recent history had been a little sad and after the war it stood neglected, occupied intermittently by the local farmer. Then it was bought by an inspirational couple, experts and collectors of tea ware, who had hoped to save it and who were now considering selling it to the Trust. My team invaded their space and looked in every cupboard and corner, taking care not to damage the magnificent collection of teapots stacked from floor to ceiling. Through the long visits they remained accommodating but insisted I keep the window shutters closed; they were afraid the geese from the nearby nature reserve would fly into the glass and destroy the collection.

Cairness was staggeringly beautiful. The great house was backed with a curious semi-circular courtyard and I would find myself caught by its presence as I walked over the lawn. The precision of its proportions made me stop and stare and, walking closer, I could see that each hard, granite block had been beautifully shaped by masons, who would have been working with the most rudimentary tools.

Robert, the gardens advisor, and I examined the remains of the designed landscape but the garden was mostly derelict with overgrown box hedging and collapsing glasshouses. Robert had started life as a gardener. He stood beside me with copies of old plans and drawings on an ancient clipboard. Then, stabbing at the images with

Entrance to Cairness House

One of the Cairness House sphinxes

Cairness House in the mid-1990s

callused fingers, he demonstrated that the garden was hugely important, perhaps as important as the house, having been designed by Thomas White, a near contemporary of Lancelot 'Capability' Brown. As we strode over the single expanse of parkland to the curving strips of woodland at the perimeter of the main park, the bones of the designed landscape were still apparent.

The team pulled together to see what might be done but the potential cost of repair was massive, and while it was definitely 'Trustworthy', the finances just did not stack up and I had to recommend against acquisition. Fortunately, restoring buyers were found and it was saved.

The reticence about new acquisitions continued. Seven years later, when I was part of the senior management team as interim director for the North East, the beautiful Dumfries House in Ayrshire was considered but not acquired.

At this time the Trust's head office was on the south side of Charlotte Square in Edinburgh. Each month I would travel south to sit in the boardroom, feeling curious and out of place. There was always a financial crisis to be wrestled with and this time was no different. Fortunately, the number crunching was ameliorated by the director of conservation, Dr Peter Burman. We were chums from the conferences we had spoken at and his analysis of Dumfries House and its incredible collection almost won the day.

The senior management met in the 'dead fish room'. On one wall hung an enormous driftwood box, within which a window revealed assorted objects as if in a crofter's window and decorated with a fish skin, which if considered from some angles as it hung lengthwise with the top folded over, especially in the more trying points of a long afternoon meeting, might suggest something a little gynaecological and not what one might expect to see.

As Peter set out his case, I found myself beginning to lament the lack of vision, the loss of a campaigning zeal and a stultifying lack of ambition. In England the National Trust had acquired the childhood homes of John Lennon and Paul McCartney. A workhouse was added and there was talk of acquiring Dungeness power station. Where had the zeal to save the un-saveable gone, I mused.

I sat quietly until the bear-like chief executive officer raised his head to peer through bushy eyebrows. 'Ian,' he asked, 'what do you think?'

I startled to wakefulness and dragged my eye from the strange fish skin. 'Well,' I said, trying to sound confident, and I hesitated, hoping this might look like deep thought. 'The Trust should be the long stop.' A grizzly eyebrow was raised towards me. 'I think the Trust is better at grasping opportunities than it is at fixing problems.' I saw quizzical looks and ploughed on.

I had been thinking about both Cairness, where the costs were prohibitive, and Ossian's Hall in the 1950s, an opportunity that had been grasped, remembering what Ben the manager had told me as we stood on the little balcony. Spence had been offered the chance to rescue the place with little funding and limited opportunity to investigate. He created a space that would require minimal maintenance and the most obvious change was a viewing platform at the end of the building. Visitors could now be exposed to the roar of the falls and the wind on their faces, as I had experienced on that stopover years before.

Ben had explained this to me as we leaned on the metal rail, which seemed thin and mean and reminded me of municipal railings, as unappealing as the industrial metal columns holding up the roof and the concrete floor. Then we walked around and I could see remnants of the eighteenth century plaster. The original entrance door was missing and an ill-fitting metal gate had been installed. If you looked closely you could just make out graffiti that had been scratched into the masonry.

Together we pondered what we should do. 'Perhaps,' I mused, 'the balcony should be removed and the building restored to its eighteenth century appearance?

Ben looked askance. 'No, no, no, no,' his English accent more pronounced as he became agitated. 'You can't do that. People love it. There would be a mutiny. Whatever we do, it has to stay.' There was a metaphorical stamping of a foot.

Restoration would have been a traditional conservation approach and I was aware of the restoration of garden buildings at Studley Royal and the Rievaulx Terrace in Yorkshire, both of which are a huge success. But Ben was right. The Spence intervention and the creation of the platform were well-established features. He had created a place that met the needs of the visitors and this simple, plain balcony could be described as a bold, modernist addition, but would anyone agree?

The wee building was quite clearly an important part of the Hermitage, but the wind and mist insinuated themselves, making it little more than a damp and muddy corridor. No visitor could understand what it was there for and it suffered. On that visit with Ben, we saw that the floor was decorated with a big circle of tyre rubber from the spinning wheels of a motorbike ridden by some overexcited youth.

I struggled at the beginning to comprehend whether the Spence period was really all that important in the history of the place. It was, and one of my less successful attempts in persuasion was when I tried to draw a somewhat strained analogy with music.

'Could the redesign of the place be Spence's string quartet?' I suggested, 'rather than his symphony, working with a limited range of instruments?' This was usually met with a puzzled expression.

Ossian's Hall, partially destroyed by protesters in 1869

Soon it seemed I could not escape pictures of the hall in calendars and magazines and they all had happy families crowded onto the balcony. That was its significance; it put the visitors just where they wanted to be.

'Look,' said Ben. 'Whatever we do, we don't want the place to be blown up again.' The front doors and surrounding masonry had been blown apart by protesters, in anger when the Duke of Atholl, the owner, introduced tolls on the new Tay Bridge nearby.

As we researched the old place, the hall began to reveal its secrets as, layer by layer, its story was laid bare. Why, I wondered was it linked to Ossian? My research led me into Gaelic lore and the works of James Macpherson, a folk tale collector and author of the poetry of Ossian. In 1760 his publication *Fragments of ancient poetry, collected in the Highlands of Scotland, and translated from the Gaelic or Erse language* became a phenomenon which even captivated Napoleon, who kept a copy with him in exile—clearly he knew his Erse from his Elba! A huge scandal would later reveal that the *Fragments* were a forgery, but Macpherson's legacy remains important. He put Gaelic literature on the world stage. It is interesting to ponder on how perceptions of authenticity in the eighteenth century are mirrored today in the tourism business. The alacrity with which the shading of history in movies and TV is used to draw in the visitor suggests that nothing is ever new.

The story of the place was teased apart by the North East archaeologist in our first ever project conservation plan and it stands today, I believe, as an exemplar of good practice. Our knowledge of the place was now such that we had to do more than just repair the damage; we had to give the hall back a little of its original flair.

Imagine you are a visitor in 1795, clutching a tattered copy of *Fragments*, stumbling off a small boat at the side of the Tay and bright in anticipation, not really knowing what to expect. The boatman encourages you into the birch and alder woods. You are from the city and well read but you know that these are dangerous places. It was only fifty years earlier that the Jacobites had run amok and Lord George Murray, one of the Jacobite generals, was a relative of the Duke.

As you make your way along a path you can hear, but not see, the river nearby. After a while a small round building with rustic stonework and a conical roof appears and the river is louder but unseen.

The boatman walks forward, a hidden door in the stone wall opens and you walk into a small round chamber. The door closes and you stand in the gloom until your eyes adjust to the light from a cupola above. A portrait of blind Ossian becomes visible before you. At this point you would probably sigh in wonder at the achievement and be satisfied, ready to move on. Suddenly, the guide pulls a hidden lever and the portrait springs to the side. A mirrored chamber lies beyond, furnished with a bay window looking out to the waterfall, and the sun shines, its light reflected by the mirrors, as the window is opened to allow the crashing noise of the waterfall to fill the room.

How, I wondered, could this surprise and wonder be recreated today? We are exposed to so much sensory overload it would be impossible. So I decided that, with a little imagination, something akin to this experience might be possible, and I appointed one of Scotland's leading creative architects, Ben Tindall.

Ben is short and bald with a big, bushy beard and likes to cycle around Edinburgh. The Edinburgh artist John Kay would no doubt have captured him in one of his satirical prints from the eighteenth century.

'Ben,' I said, handing over our conservation plan, 'we want the balcony to stay, and we want to bring back surprise and wonder for the visitor and make it clean and dry for weddings… if anyone wants to tie the knot over the waterfall.'

My approach with creative and talented people like Ben it is to give them space. What would be the point in imposing caveats and conditions that inhibit the very attributes you admire?

I travelled to his idiosyncratic studio tucked behind Edinburgh Castle and, after a climb, sat at the big table in his office. Ben bustled in and fixed me with sharp, perceptive eyes. The walls were lined with well-thumbed books and we spoke about the Hall.

'Well,' whispered Ben through his whiskers, eyes glittering and eyebrows bobbing. 'Let's see what can be done.'

After a while he said, 'There's a real opportunity here to be novel, creative and imaginative. You know the Trust can be a little dusty. Let's do something amazing.' Slowly a feeling of dread came upon me, a sinking feeling, as the costs rose way beyond the budget. My face paled and I wondered what to do.

Back up in leafy Perthshire I saw the other Ben. 'An appeal?' he suggested. 'Everybody loves the place.'

Fingal and Conban-Cargla, by Calum Colvin (1961-) (Calum Colvin)

ABOVE AND BOTTOM LEFT:
Ossian's Hall interior
(Benjamin Tindall Architects)

BOTTOM RIGHT: Calum Colvin
(Benjamin Tindall Architects)

Ben the manager was the energetic face of the Trust in Perthshire, so meetings were held, letters sent out and the slow trickle of small donations became a flood.

Ben the architect now got to work, first designing the sliding door that should spring into the wall. Then inspiration struck; Ossian would be reinstated on the sliding door. The mirrored walls might be re-imagined with pictures on a reflective metal background.

We needed an artist who would create something wonderful, someone who would have the stature within the creative community to match the exceptional architecture of the place.

Ben the architect began the search, and Calum Colvin was the man. Calum is exceptional, working out of Dundee and Edinburgh in an almost unique photographic

Ossian's Hall, new door

trompe-l'oeil style. The two Bens and I travelled to see him work. His place was filled with cameras and stuff he had created for earlier works. I saw piles of plastic chairs and concrete blocks assembled on a stage before a massive camera and my face must have shown my confusion. 'Look through the lens,' he said and before me the random assembly morphed into an image of Ossian singing. This amazing composition would be the image for the sliding door.

The contractors arrived in 2006 and the wind tunnel that the Hall had become was transformed by the insertion of glass doors at the falls, forcing visitors to stop and ponder as they made their way to the waterfall, and the addition of a timber door at the entrance.

On the day of the opening I wandered with the crowds to the Hall and watched as its round facade stumped them. The new door was crafted to mimic the masonry and painted to replicate the pattern of lichens and mosses on the walls. Eventually they discovered the door and entered the first chamber.

In the gloom, the portrait of Ossian on the door stopped them until the handle was pulled and it slid away to reveal the main chamber. The walls were dark with blood red paint and the new murals glinted in the reflected light. The opening to the balcony was fitted with huge glass doors and Calum's stunning artwork was further complimented by Gaelic poetry by Aonghas MacNeacail.

We all hoped that this chapter in the history of the hall would send it happily forward. Old buildings are sterile without people and the impressions they take with them, or in some cases leave behind them. If on exiting you look closely at the graffiti scratched into the masonry you might be puzzled by the spelling. Here and there are words in Polish left by soldiers of World War II who camped nearby. Their children now visit to see this reminder of a difficult past.

What about the Spence balcony?

It is still there, unaltered.

THIS·SAME·JESUS WHICH·IS·TAKEN·UP·FROM·YOU INTO·HEAVEN·SHALL·SO·COME·IN·LIKE MANNER·AS·YE·HAVE·SEEN HIM·GO·INTO·HEAVEN

9

ADAM AND THE HAPPY MASONS

At Christmas 1987 I was at home when my phone rang and Mrs Stanger, the long-serving housekeeper at Haddo, called to say that there was water in the entrance hall. This was a little worrying as the entrance is two floors below the roof. 'I took away that wee drawing of the house,' she told me. 'The back's a bit wet but there a lot mair water now.' She was referring to William Adam's original plans of the house from 1733.

I rushed over to find a waterfall pouring over the wallpaper and disappearing under the floor.

The cascade was coming from melting snow on the roof that had found its way through the old lead when the outlet was filled with ice and the melt water had nowhere to go but inside and down where, as I stood in wonder, it was now soaking away into the ground below the flooring.

It took five years to stop this from happening again, and the work was completed in late 1992, when the roof was finally repaired, just in time for another Christmas. All that remained was to put the flagpole back, and I nearly died in the attempt.

Adam Wilkin, the foreman leadworker, asked me to lend a hand getting the pole vertical and we had just got it up after a bit of a struggle. I stepped back in relief and realised my heel was now on the edge, over a 20m drop. I felt an iron grip on my wrist and Adam looked as startled as I was, but he gave me a hefty pat on the shoulder and we got down.

Raising the flagpole at this time was the final act in the repair of the roof. It had to be put back in time for the festivities, hosted by Lady Aberdeen, widow of the last owner. These culminated in 'drams and reels' in the library on Hogmanay. I think that is what she called them; I had to pay close attention as she spoke in a husky whisper. Sometimes I could only tell that she was speaking because I could see her lips moving slightly.

That Yule torrent in 1987 was not the first big leak. In previous years there had been many through the ancient leadwork and at one point in 1978 part of the ceiling in the dining room had fallen down when water poured through from the bay window above. That was the first year of Trust ownership.

Haddo House Chapel east window

As we stood watching the flood, Mrs Stanger, who could have been Adam's sister from her appearance and manner, was unflappable. 'You stop the leak and I'll clean it up,' she said.

Ethyl Stanger was of my mother's generation and I would never use her first name. She had been with the house for decades, and her activities were astonishing and varied. She was the only cleaner at the time and in addition baked cakes for the tearoom in those early Trust years. She made and served refreshments at events in the house and looked after the hats and coats at the annual Haddo Ball, among her many duties. She was and is a great supporter of her local community, where she regularly won accolades for her baking at the Women's Rural Institute. I have a confession to make here. In 1983 I stayed for a while at Haddo in the room below the kitchen where the cakes were made. At night the smell was irresistible and I would sneak upstairs. Later, guiltily, I would put a small donation in the 'honesty box'.

We got the place dry and the rooms back together and I had the whole place surveyed in the summer of 1988. The lead on the roof had to be replaced. The roof is enormous, probably equivalent to a football pitch-sized area of lead, mostly laid around 1890 but with a selection of later work from the 1930s.

It was here I found the most toxic substance known to man, or at least, known to me.

I had invited the venerable designer of leadwork, Richard Murdoch, senior technical officer of the Lead Sheet Association and author of the lead sheet manual, to give some advice. Richard was a dapper cockney, always seen in a trench coat, garrulous and generous with his knowledge. We came to know each other quite well from meeting at conferences.

On that first visit we decided to start at the south end of the house, where old Lady A. lived. So we got in and were assailed as usual by the fearsome Westies and the smell of boiled cabbage from the huge kitchen that served her and her many guests. Then up to the bedrooms and out through a window, catching shins on window sills before standing on the flat roof. We were on the laundry wing, where below us huge sinks and pulleys remained, though they were no longer used. This area of lead covered an area about a tennis court in size, to maintain the sports ground analogy.

Richard seemed excited, in the way that trainspotters might be at the sight of a rare diesel engine on a small provincial line. 'Look.' he squeaked. 'Pinholes'. He had an accent more likely to be heard within the sound of Bow Bells than leafy Aberdeenshire. I peered at the surface and sure enough the lead was pockmarked with many tiny holes.

'What was this part of the building used for?' he asked.

'The laundry,' I said.

'Ah, ha!' he said. 'This roof is failing from the inside out.'

The hot damp air in the laundry had condensed on the underside of the lead. Condensed water is corrosive to lead and had been eating away at it. We peeled a bit back and found a thick layer of white powder.

'There it is,' he drawled. 'Lead oxide. Toxic, so don't touch.'

Lead oxide should not be touched with bare hands so we pushed the lead back down. A local plumbing firm got the repair contract, mainly because they had a superb leadworker, Adam. He was over sixty and, like nearly all tradesmen of his generation, wore a cap and had a cigarette permanently dangling from his mouth or pinched and placed behind his ear. He wore Scotland's other national costume, the boiler

Adam Wilkin

suit, and a small, tightly knotted tie peeked over the bib at his neck like a swan neck at the top of a rainwater pipe.

Among his peers he was not unusual in his appearance and manner. These Aberdonian chaps are often fairly short and heavily built with broad faces and a taciturn approach to life, and they speak Doric, the local dialect. I sometimes wonder if they are descendants of the Picts, who fought the Romans and left us the hill forts and the intricately carved monoliths scattered around Aberdeenshire.

'Well, it looks like I'll never hae till handle another pipe,' said Adam. He could see this job lasting till he retired, which it did.

He would arrive in the early morning, long before a laggard like me got out there, and he worked at a slow but steady pace that never wavered through the day, driving his apprentices mad with frustration. One day he beckoned to me and, peering over the wall onto the roof, he drew from his pocket a nail made from lead hidden in the roof, probably by his lads. He was quite taken in and would show it to anyone, wondering who would need a nail made from soft lead. The boys would smirk behind him and I kept the secret, or maybe that joke had been on me.

Haddo was in a great bustle at the time. I had the funding and the wind at my back, which, combined with the confidence of youth, meant there were craftsmen everywhere. We were not only fixing the roof at the time. At the bottom of the scaffolding were two masons working to repair old mortar on the building. Water had been insidiously sneaking in through the stonework in the chapel, where the masonry was being slowly destroyed.

Time has erased the names of those masons from my memory but one worked on the rubble areas, which were the main walls of the house, and the other worked on the ashlar fine joints at the windows and on the chapel.

Rubble mason and I stood at the foot of the north wing, where he was creating a new washed recessed joint, just as I had asked for. The technique was the preferred way to do repairs to ancient monuments back in those days. It made the stones prominent and the mortar was carefully brushed and washed to make the tiny pieces of gravel appear like raisins in a fruit scone. It is no longer the way we would do this today.

We looked at the way the wall was put together and I said, pointing, 'What do you think those pebbles were for?' These walls often had small stones pushed into the mortar, known as cherry cocking.

'These eens,' he said, tapping some trapped between the big stones with his trowel, 'stop the big eens rocking when ye put one on anither.' He mimicked the act of trying to get an irregular block to sit on top of another. 'It would rock about and the little eens keep it level.' His arms rocked about as he mimed holding a heavy boulder, shoulders hunched. 'The mortar's no glue. It's soft and just fills in the spaces between the big steens.'

'Then why put those other smaller ones in?' I asked, pointing at some that clearly did not perform that function. He took off his hard hat and looked puzzled. Then we realised that lime mortar tends to crack as it dries if the surface area is too big. Cherry cocking reduces the volume and surface area of lime mortar and helps reduce the risk of cracking.

Ashlar mason was toiling away at the walls of the chapel, finely packing away metre after metre of mortar with a smile on his face. His Doric was impenetrable. The chapel is about a hundred and fifty years younger than the mansion, and the laird had decided that instead of the restrained Palladian style elsewhere, Gothic was better, complete with massive stained glass windows replete with scriptural imagery. The principal window on the east gable has the apostles gathered around Christ, rising in majesty up, up, through clouds to a blue yonder.

A few years earlier I was rewiring the chapel and looked up. The windows tinkled and rattled in the wind as the leadwork buckled under the weight of the glass. This drew my gaze to the paint on the glass and I noticed that it had begun to disappear, allowing the light to stream in, unfiltered, while condensation trickled down. The grey

Ashlar mason at Haddo House

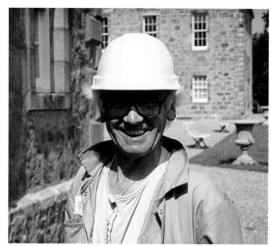

Rubble mason at Haddo House

Martin Farrelly working on the chapel windows

Aberdonian sky could be viewed where once celestial clouds had drifted over the halos of the assembled apostles.

Stained glass craftspeople were hard to find and a search only revealed makers of decorative gewgaws to hang in your kitchen window, perhaps with an image of a robin in the snow or a pretty flower. After a call for help, a charming Irish craftsman came along. Martin had worked at Pluscardine Abbey and now was in a studio not far away.

He was deaf but could speak well, having lost his hearing as a child, and he had an infectious enthusiasm. He lip-read and peered with intensity and humour when you spoke. His leadworking was superb and looking up at the apostles he challenged me. 'Now then,' his Gaelic lilt obvious, 'how can ye tell which of the bunch is John?' As a child in working-class Glasgow, I had avoided all religion thanks to my atheist father, and I stood in ignorance until he told me the answer. 'He is the one without a beard; he never has any whiskers at all.'

Soon the first windows were out and on his bench, and a small group of apprentices worked with him. Sadly he decided to retire before we had completed the main window and he moved to a lovely part of Deeside. I sought other craftsmen and found them in Kilmarnock, and soon the windows were all back in place.

Old Lady Aberdeen decided that the chapel should have a special service of rededication. The Archbishop of Canterbury was asked but was unavailable, so the Primus of the Scottish Episcopal Church came in his stead. Up on the roof, the family flag was raised in celebration and no one fell off.

Eventually Adam and the masons finished and set off for new jobs, or in Adam's case, into a semi-retirement from which he would be called back to dress some complex lead shape on occasion. He could be seen from time to time over the years in the market town, cigarette and bunnet in place, moving with that same deliberate and purposeful steady walk, free of his boiler suit but with his tie still neatly knotted.

10
FIRST NATIONS

In April 2009 I was on a crowded commuter train going into Perth. Not Perth by the silvery Tay, but Perth in Western Australia, far from the castles and hills of the Trust. I had been asked to travel there to develop and share my skills, if I could.

Each day, while I was briefly supporting the National Trust down under, I would take this crowded train into town. As I stood on the suburban platform among tidy, detached homes, each with a neat lawn and a barbeque, the sun always shone and I realised just how different life could be if you did not have to wonder if you might need an umbrella, or shiver as you stepped over the threshold in the morning.

On this particular morning, an Aboriginal family got on the train and stood near me, and a small incident caused me to pay much more attention to the tribulations of this First Nation for the remainder of my stay.

My home in Perth was at Guildford on the southern edge of the city, close to the outback, and as I made my way around the city I would often see these sad and desperate people, slumped at the roadside or propped against a wall. There was a sense of quiet desperation, not unlike the Glasgow of my youth, where unemployed, aged men would sit crumpled under their greatcoats with their bunnets before them, begging for small change on George V Bridge. Neither of these sights had been part of my experience in Aberdeenshire, where farming, fishing and oil had been a cushion for the rural poor.

The small group on the train were clearly the worse for wear, solvents and plastic bags being their oblivion of choice, but they were doing no one any harm. The crowd swayed as the train approached a station and I was jostled as a young Aussie pushed his way through to grab hold of the Aboriginals, then, with a sharp tug and a push as the doors opened, forcibly eject them. They stood on the platform looking lost while everyone stared at their feet and the man exploded with a few expletives. The train moved away and I watched them fade into the distance.

A few days later Tom, the tall American CEO of the Trust in Perth WA, called over to me. 'Hey, it's about time you went into the outback. You'll love Kalgoorlie. It's filled with blood-and-spit miners.' Kalgoorlie is located 595 kilometres east-north-east of Perth, at the end of the Great Eastern highway. How could I refuse?

The Flow of Energy by Rande Cook (1977-) (IMD)

Soon I was meandering along the desert highway to inspect a building halfway to the gold mine town. It was a dilapidated pump house near the settlement of Southern Cross, one of a string of such villages created as stopovers in the days before fast cars. This structure was part of the 'Golden Pipeline', a nineteenth century cast iron water main that ran across the surface of the desert to the boomtowns of the gold rush.

The task I was addressing was not overly challenging and I had plenty of time, so I set off to see an Aboriginal site, Mulka's Cave. Mulka, it turned out, was a legendary character, cursed and unable to hunt properly, who turned to cannibalism. It did not look far on the map but was three hours in the car over rutted, unsurfaced roads. You had to keep your wits about you, as the only difference between the road and the desert was the tyre tracks and the occasional sign.

The cave turned out to be a tumble of enormous pebble-shaped boulders that had been deposited there by some ferocious geological event. I was on my own and followed the signposts on foot. The wind got up and a little sand got into the air and my eyes. The eucalyptus trees were waving wildly as I walked through them to get to the cave.

I stretched out my hand through the dusty air to lean on a boulder while sand blew around in tiny whirlwinds and my eyes watered when I peered under one of the giant stones. The cave roof was covered with ancient red ochre handprints. Squeezing through a small gap, I sat on a stone and held my own hand up, not touching anything. The prints were about half the size of mine. The floor around me was covered with tumbled rubble and the back of the cave was open. I crawled over to see more prints and got out at the back with another squeeze. I felt an unwelcoming chill in the warm desert air and quickly left for the long drive back through a wild sandstorm, taking care not to lose myself.

A day later I drove into Kalgoorlie, the main street lined with fairly unappealing houses, till in the centre the remnants of the gold rush were visible in the wrought iron of the hotels and bars. A little further and I found a gigantic hole in the ground from which the gold is still extracted. The scale of this opening is hard to describe. It looked as if a small mountain had been lifted from the earth, turned over and pressed into the sands of the desert leaving an inverted impression of itself. As you peer down you can see tiny lorries that slowly wind their way up the side of the pit and turn out to be the size of a bungalow with tyres taller than me.

Tom did not exaggerate; it is still a bit of a frontier town with wild young miners and bars staffed by scantily clad young women, and there are nightly fights. It reminded me of Sauchiehall Street in the 1970s.

Aboriginal people wander through the town, mostly in a poor condition but apparently without the desperation I saw in Perth. Among the visitor attractions was a house in a back street where you could buy their art and crafts and inside lived a chap who acquired them from the people who arrived at his door. If you wanted to find a caricature Aussie, then here he was, short, in his sixties, unshaven under his bush hat, baggy shorts, skinny legs and heavy boots.

The night I stayed in the miners' hotel was filled with the sounds of drunken brawling and in the morning the pavement and wall of the hotel were splattered with blood, so I set off back to Perth.

Shortly after this I was asked if I would like to represent the Trust at an event in Albany, on the south coast. It was at an Aboriginal fish trap, in the form of a low-walled enclosure in an azure lagoon. The fish were caught in the enclosure as the tide ebbed, and carbon dating of shells built into the wall suggested it was over 7,500 years old.

I flew down in a small aircraft and the pilot was a tall, ageing Aussie who let me sit in the front. He told me of the time he had taken food relief into Papua New Guinea during a local emergency. One day he landed in the forest clearing to find fewer people than he expected waiting for the food parcels, so he handed out what he had and they each got a bit more than usual. Next time the place was crowded with a large and hopeful group expecting the generosity to continue.

When this did not occur there was a lot of shouting and pushing until one chap in a loincloth with colourful feathers and piercings stepped forward and launched his spear at the pilot. It landed between his feet.

'What did you do?' I asked.

'I shot him.' My eyebrows disappeared into my scalp. 'With salt. I've still got that spear on the wall.'

Albany fish traps (IMD)

When we landed in Albany the sun was beating down and as I approached the coast I could see someone standing on the surface of the water about 100 metres out in the lagoon. It took a moment to realise he was perched on the stone walls of the fish trap and he was casting his line into the pool where the fish were trapped. A cool breeze drifted over the place and within a few minutes a small group gathered for the ceremony. I looked around the company. There were no Aboriginals to be seen. The local community had gone 'walkabout' and were no longer there.

Their nomadic lifestyle continues and government support with farms or other employment tends to fail as they head out when there is a death in the community or a festival or ceremony to attend, often, I was informed, leaving their crops untended. This gives the Aboriginals a poor reputation with the new Australians and a downward spiral of misunderstanding is assured.

I was invited to a seminar on Aboriginal culture that was aimed at oil executives whose companies engage with the First Nation when they need to use their land. The first speaker took us on a journey through the decline in indigenous language. She spotted the Scot in the audience and recalled that many settlers noticed a similarity with our pronunciation and asked me to pronounce words with an 'R'. I took on the music hall stereotype with glee and emphasised the rolling sound, parodying Scottie from *Star Trek* to embed the caricature in the minds of the delegates.

She revealed that when Captain Cook arrived at Botany Bay there were an estimated 600 languages spoken across the continent. There are now about twenty and most are spoken only by a few individuals.

Rottnest Island off Perth is now a holiday resort but had been a penal colony for Aboriginals and I had the chance to visit. A swift hydrofoil takes you from Fremantle across the sea to a long pier filled with happy trippers and the small settlement nearby

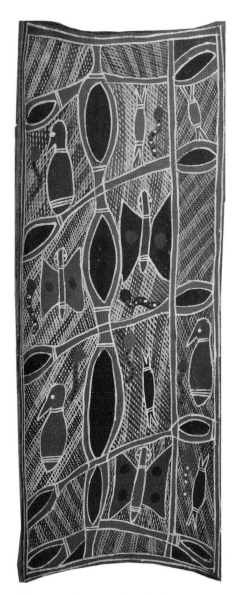

Aboriginal West Arnhem bark painting by indigenous artist Benny Muduruk (1930-c.1990) (IMD)

has some of the oldest buildings on the west coast. The prison is a polygonal structure enclosing a courtyard where the cells had become holiday flats. I noticed an area of rough ground nearby which had been roped off. This enclosed hundreds of unmarked graves that had recently been discovered. It is hardly surprising that the holidaymakers do not include anyone from the Aboriginal community. The National Trust of Western Australia have been leaders in developing programmes to address a little of this horrible heritage, and I was deeply moved to learn about it.

A couple of years later Tom invited me to support him at the International National Trust Conference, in Victoria, Vancouver, Canada. I found myself in another small plane, this time flying over pine-filled rocky islets to Vancouver Island. We stayed in a massive Victorian hotel near a harbour filled with huge ferries and pleasure craft of every description.

The conference was opened by the chief of the First Nation people of Victoria, an erudite man whose political skills helped ensure that his community prospered as much as possible. I was invited to visit a 'reservation', which turned out to be a rather elegant housing estate on the coast with amazing views across to lots of other islands, well covered with pine trees.

The salmon were running and the eagles were well fed. This community had an air of comfortable unity despite their justified grievance at their loss of land and influence. The greatest risk to their cultural unity is the overwhelming attractiveness of the North American lifestyle to the young people.

The museum in Victoria, British Columbia, is not far from the harbour. Its staff were kindly ladies and within are giant, brown totem poles, their images in earth paints fading into the gloom of the conservation lighting and remnants of clothes and farm tools. They are displayed alongside stories of death and disaster from the disease the west brought.

The art of the Victoria First Nation was to be seen everywhere, from totem poles to fine art prints. A little conversation with the locals helped me to understand that this culture, decimated by smallpox in the late nineteenth century, had a resilience that helped it survive. I heard about their wars with Russia over otter pelts, and their victory. They could not resist the tide of immigrants and, as in Australia, there had been a policy of forced integration, with children removed to boarding schools where abuse was endemic, but their ability to hold on to their culture helped them endure.

The contrast with Perth was stark.

11

STRAWBERRIES AND PEACHES

It was 1986 and Castle Fraser was on fire. It was just a wee fire and not too bad as these things go, but it was a stiffener nonetheless for me and the curious cast of characters inhabiting the place and its surroundings. The minute I heard about the fire, I rushed over to inspect the damage.

Normally the journey to Castle Fraser was a pleasant trip through the shire, driving along the river Dee with Bennachie appearing on the horizon as the road twists and turns before ascending a gentle hill to the castle, sitting among fields and surrounded by low hills at the end of a long avenue of ancient trees. At that time the Trust only operated the castle, garden and a tiny package of land, and the rest remained with Major and Mrs Smiley, the generous and kindly donors, who lived in the nearby stables and maintained a keen and sometimes proprietorial interest in the castle.

As I hurried that morning through the narrow country roads to get to the place, expecting to see a smoking pyre, I crested the hill before the castle but there was no smoke rising. 'Phew,' I thought. 'At least it's not the castle.'

The conflagration had been in one of the small gatehouses, which had lost its roof. Castle Strawberry had survived. 'Fraise' is the Norman French strawberry flower emblem the ancient forebears adopted, and its images can be seen on some of the dormer windows.

As I had expected, Bill M. the gardener, a taciturn former farmer and kirk elder, was waiting to meet me and begin the clear-up.

Now Bill was a sturdy chiel. He had created the garden he managed for the Trust over just six years and to my untrained eye it appeared mature and colourful. He always seemed to have completed a full day's work by mid-morning, ready for the visitors to arrive, and he would continue to graft, with his sleeves rolled up to his elbows, right through the day. Like so many men of his generation, his work clothes were effectively from the same drawer as his Sunday best. Tradesmen took their skills seriously and the more experienced you were the less workmanlike you wanted to appear. My father had been the same. His trade was in printing, as a compositor, now a long-dead craft, and his only concession to work wear was to remove the collar from his shirt. Those collars

Castle Fraser by James Giles RSA (1801-1870)

Castle Fraser gatehouses in winter, 1920s

were designed to be detached and reattached by inserting tiny studs with mother-of-pearl heads, like cufflinks.

Bill's garden, now a joy to everyone, had been an empty shell after the former owners had removed most of the plants when the castle came to the Trust. 'Well, fit can ye dee?' he would say when I raised an eyebrow at this. 'Ye just get on wi it.' Over the years the place bloomed, fruit grew and paths appeared. He was even able to sell plants to augment his small budget.

Bill's empire was the Walled Garden, unusual in being built from clay bricks, as most garden walls in Aberdeenshire are granite. Bill would sniff and take me to look at it. 'This wall was heated,' he explained as we looked at the crumbling bricks. 'If ye take oot some of they bricks ye'll see they're about a fit long.' He pulled one out of the wall and I could see that it helped form a flue through the wall that would have carried hot gases from the boilers to keep the wall warm and protect the plants from frost.

The long-gone gardeners before Bill had fixed support wires on the wall for the bushes and tied them to nails driven into it. Bill would also pound nails into the joints between the bricks but the old mortar was too soft and so he patched them in cement, which only caused the bricks to crumble more quickly. He could see that this was a problem and took time to help me develop some proposals for its repair. Bill retired before we could get started but I brought in masons from a local firm, even though they had little experience in working on old buildings.

As work began, I explained that I wanted them to remove the cement mortar that had been used to patch the wall by using a tool known as a plugging chisel. It is shaped to facilitate mortar removal, and the grooved part, or 'flute', of the chisel is designed to allow any remains to be removed. This is really a plasterer's tool and has a shape that stops too much damage being caused to the bricks when the cement is taken out. Alex, a grey-haired mason, looked puzzled. 'Ae? Fit's that?' He did not recognise the name, which being young

Castle Fraser Garden wall mortar removal

and green I had taken from a textbook, so I did a little sketch with his stubby pencil on, literally, a fag packet.

His head rose from the sketch to reveal a face suffused with comprehension and a slight air of condescension. He looked at me as if at a daft lad, which I was, and said, 'Oh! A dookin iron.' I had used the English, not the Scottish, terminology. A 'dook' in Scots is a hole cut in a wall to take a piece of wood that supports plaster lath. It can also mean the wood itself. In England this is a plug. 'Iron' in this context can also be used to mean 'tool'. Alex was now on my side and we had quite a few chats about the past. I spoke to him about working in lime and how that work would have to be stopped in winter. He looked interested. 'That'll be where the auld saying's frae, then,' he said.

I thought he was meaning the standard phrase, 'Ne'er cast a cloot till May is oot.'

'Naw,' he said. 'When the wife went tae the shop in spring she would sae till the man, "It's the 31st of March. Ye can kiss my arse. My auld man's a mason," meaning he got back to work at that time and the winter's debts could be cleared.'

Up at the castle, Mrs Lavinia Smiley, and her father before her, had loved the old place. For many years they had sought the original house under the layers of Georgian and Victorian decoration, carefully removing those newer layers in their search for the authentic ancient building. They appeared to seek a rugged fortification under the wallpaper and plaster, perhaps unaware that the house of the early seventeenth century had been of significant sophistication, though since covered by the fashions of succeeding generations. The enthusiasm for these investigations and the re-imagining of the interior culminated when the place was given to the Trust in 1976. There could be a little tension at times with the Trust in the years that followed, and the distance that created meant I never heard their reaction to the small but destructive fire, but I suspect they would have been quite distressed at the loss.

Sadly, a few years later, in 1993, the estate was dissolved on the death, within months of each other, of both husband and wife and the maternal link that Mrs

The stables at Castle Fraser

Smiley had maintained with the place was lost. She had been a creative force whose enthusiasm for the place and artistic interests were to be seen in the slightly stark castle interior and the many books she wrote. For Lavinia, the castle was a giant dolls' house and she would acquire interesting pieces to dress it from time to time.

When part of the remaining estate was sold, the Trust acquired the fields and the stables around the castle but unfortunately not the Bronze Age remnants of a recumbent stone circle close by—one of the best in Aberdeenshire, with six stones still standing. The North East can boast a higher concentration of stone circles and other megalithic remains than almost any other region of the British Isles, with around a hundred known sites in Aberdeenshire alone.

After the sale, the old estate office was developed to house the Trust regional staff, including me, and the Smiley home was divided into three apartments. Walking through it, I found those poignant remnants of family life that I often find when a property changes hands. Children's heights marked on door posts, scorch marks where a hot pan was placed on a kitchen top, scuff marks under coat hangers, worn patches on carpets. You can read the history of a family in such detritus. Small items found here and there speak of personal foibles; matches, ashtrays, old newspapers and paperback books sit beside empty flower vases stained from the water and stems they once held.

Their home filled most of the hexagonal building, which dates from the late eighteenth century. The walls in the courtyard were covered with plum trees and on the south side there was even a peach. The Smileys, or maybe Bill the gardener, must have had great powers to entice peaches without a glasshouse in central Aberdeenshire. There was a small, disused swimming pool nearby under a rough glasshouse roof and a sauna in one of their rooms, both very exotic in Aberdeenshire at the time.

Espaliered peach trees on the south side of the courtyard

The changes happened quickly and the apartments were soon let out. The pool became a car park for tenants and the sauna was removed to accommodate the expanded office. Meanwhile the Trust curator looked on with quiet dismay and likened the effect to the Britons moving into a villa after the Romans had left.

A few years later, the children of Major and Mrs Smiley worked with me to display some artefacts from their years there, in a small exhibition near the top of the round tower, but this did not happen without a hitch.

They very kindly supplied wallpaper for the room to complement the items that were to be displayed. It had a pattern of foliage and branches on a yellow background, brought in from France. When papering any room the pattern should be centred on a key feature, such as a fireplace. This room had a fireplace but it was off-centre on the wall. The paper-hanger had thought hard and determined that the arrangement of door, window and fireplace meant that there was no key feature, so he had not centred the pattern over the mantelpiece, and on completion it looked odd, but we fixed that at the second attempt.

Thinking back to that morning in 1986, it was fun putting the roof back on that wee gatehouse, but I made a small error that is still visible today. If you look at any traditional ridge stone on a slated roof you will see it is an inverted 'V', cut to fit neatly on the apex of the pitched roof. The thin edge of the stone that sits over the slates should be cut at an angle to prevent a shadow being formed. I did not know this and made a drawing with the edge to be cut square, which I gave to a stone cutter near Elgin, the owner of an old, established family firm. He did what was asked and the stones are there today, shadow and all. I am sure no one notices, but it irritates me. Oh well, I think as I watch the visitors walk down from the car park towards the restored gatehouses. It could have been a lot worse.

12

THE AUNTIES

The little fire at Castle Fraser pales beside the conflagration in 1966, when part of Crathes Castle burned down. I heard about this from many of the characters who were there at the time and who remained.

They saw the loss of the Queen Anne wing and its Victorian bits, which had been home to Jamie Burnett of Leys, the youthful laird. Fortunately the old tower house was almost untouched. Philip the forester was one of the first on the scene and, in the thickest of thick Doric, he told me the fire brigade arrived from Banchory, Aberdeen and all the little stations from smaller towns nearby.

Crathes was perhaps fortunate in being located on the road to Balmoral and maybe the authorities were more ready to deal with a fire in a historic building than elsewhere. The next day, as the smoke rose from the damp, roofless ruin, the place was surrounded by men from the Trust in their greatcoats and trilbies. Among them was the Trust consultant architect, Schomberg Scott, who was brought in to deal with the disaster.

This was one of the first places I was taken to visit in 1983 by the factor, Mike, who drove me out there at terrifying speed around convoluted single-track roads in his Ford Escort. Waiting for us was Anne Murray, the resident property manager, or 'representative', as these custodians were known—nothing so prosaic as 'manager'. Now living in Schomberg's new wing, she was a retired schoolteacher who presided over the property and its visitors with a dominie's firm hand. She was even known to have fingernail inspections for the room guides each day before the place opened.

Anne was not unusual. Trust property managers at that time were often either ladies of a certain age or retired officers from the forces, well versed in the curiosities of life and a hoot to be with. Crathes was ruled by a triumvirate of imposing women and a kindly head gardener. They were Anne, Betty Moir in the shop and Liz Nixon in the restaurant.

Betty controlled the shop from behind the counter. Small and bespectacled with well-permed dark hair and a bustling efficient manner, she would decorate the shop for special occasions, enticing return visits from her loyal clientele. She laughed a lot, with a deep chesty cough that only a lifelong smoker of untipped full-strength cigarettes can

Crathes Castle (Jim Henderson)

Top left: Crathes Castle before the fire
Top right: Crathes Castle after the fire
Bottom left: Schomberg Scott's reconstruction drawing

manage. Alongside her at the counter was Ellie, an octogenarian tenant from Drum Castle where she lived in the brewhouse flat. Ellie was like a wee plum duff, with white hair tied in a bun, just like the fairy godmother to Cinderella. My usual greeting on entering the shop was to ask loudly, 'Fit like, Ellie. How's your granny?' We would enjoy a laugh at the faces of the visitors, who would not know that a granny is a cowl on a chimney. Ellie's flat was always a bit smoky.

Betty liked colourful pottery and she loved jewellery. Both passions were satisfied in the Crathes shop, and she was tremendously excited when a local but internationally feted silversmith, Malcolm Appleby, began to sell some items there.

I put a display cabinet into the shop for his works and he would stock it himself while dressed in his fantastic multi-coloured and patched woolly jumper—a famous item he refers to as 'that darned jumper'—sparkling with his creations pinned haphazardly over it. He lived in the old railway station near the castle and among other things rebuilt the lost signal box, for his own amusement. There was a whimsical side to his character and on my first visit to see him I had to use the overgrown road to the old station

platform. The drive through the woodland to the disused railway line was decorated with 'molehills' and as you drove by each one they would get smaller, revealing, bit by bit, a series of plastic teddy bears. His workshop was a clutter of tools, stuff he collected and his beautiful drawings. This grotto sadly disappeared when he married and moved to Perthshire.

The final formidable lady in the triumvirate was Liz, in the restaurant, who had been there since the 1950s. Liz's food was wonderful, in a Scottish Maw Broon style. Huge steak pies would be lifted steaming from ancient gas ovens, piles of creamy mashed potatoes and sticky puddings too. Throughout the day scones and pastries would send their aroma out to entice the hungry visitor. Her restaurant was in the old horsemill, where a little of the original interior remained. It was a traditional Scottish eatery and loved by everyone who dined there.

Anne, Betty and Liz, not forgetting Ellie, were like a clutch of fussy aunts.

The family feeling at Crathes encouraged me to write the first castle survey that Historic Scotland received from the Trust. I was twenty-four and didn't turn in a well-crafted report, but Anne was very interested in the survey and we would tour the place to see where the damp was or where there was faulty wiring. We climbed the turnpike stair with Anne tapping the wall listening for a hollow sound that might suggest a hidden cupboard. She was convinced there was silver hidden within the walls, though I have yet to find it. She looked forward to the rewiring of the stairs, where she was convinced something would be discovered under the plaster, in a section which appeared to be patched. I opened it but there was nothing to be found.

Several rooms in Crathes have curious names such as Nine Nobles, Green Lady's and Muses, and they are the great treasure of the castle, with remnants of the sixteenth century decoration that was rediscovered in the nineteenth century when the plaster ceilings were taken down. Jamie Burnett's Victorian ancestors had repainted the ceilings to enhance the decorative effect, changing the colour scheme quite dramatically. If you are in these rooms you will see that the main body of the ceiling is very bright, but around the edges, at the walls, the colours are more subdued. The Trust revealed these areas in the 1950s by removing wall plaster that the Victorians had left untouched. That is the original decoration and the more colourful areas are Victorian over-painting. The paints do not work well together and the later, highly colourful paint is unstable and can flake off, which has been a conservation challenge for many years.

The horsemill restaurant

Ian Hodgkinson

Anne and I went into the Green Lady's room on one of our tours, where the ghost is said to roam. In one corner there is an oak door on the external wall, as if to a cupboard. 'Look,' said Anne, opening the door and revealing a concrete block wall. The doorway, which had been a way through to the Queen Anne wing, had been blocked after the fire. Anne pointed to the ceiling where the heat from the conflagration had scorched it, peeling back the vibrant decoration. 'If this had caught, the whole place would have burned.'

In 1967, the Trust set up the Stenhouse Conservation Centre with the particular intent of caring for these ceilings and using that knowledge for the benefit of others. It was taken over by the Department of the Environment and the centre remains part of the government agency. Until recently was based in Stenhouse Mansion, a Trust house close to Saughton Prison in Edinburgh.

The great period for conserving the ceilings was in the late 1950s and early 1960s, when the wall plaster was removed from the most decorative rooms at Crathes to reveal the earlier subdued decoration at the ends of the ceiling timbers. This encouraged the Trust to allow one of the rooms, the Muses room, to be repainted in the original colour scheme. Johnnie Morgan, the Trust joiner, a quietly spoken, kindly tradesman, told me of the approach taken by my predecessor as surveyor. 'Mr Sharp wanted me to cover the auld beams with balsa wood, that wid then be painted,' he explained, 'but he wisna happy for it being ower neat, so I had tae take a chisel tae it tae make look a bittie older.'

Anne and I, during our peregrinations, looked into the old bathroom half way up the tower. There was plaster on the floor and pipes sticking out of the walls. 'We have been waiting years for this to be fixed,' she told me. Burst pipes had revealed a ceiling in its original colours, unimproved by the Victorian Burnetts. I took a few more years to gather support for opening the room to the public, but we managed to do so in the early 1990s.

As you climb up to this room the turnpike stair stops, creating a small landing at the door, and there is a carved wooden newel post to grab as you haul yourself up. This is a post that has been reused from a canopied bed and it appears to be laburnum. There is

Original and Victorian colours in the Nine Nobles room at Crathes Castle

Ceiling of the Muses Room at Crathes Castle

another on the stair at the other side of the building. Laburnum seems to be a peculiarly Scottish favourite for furniture of that period.

I learned this from the director of Stenhouse, Rab Snowden, who was something of a legend in the Scottish conservation world. He was a sturdy loon with a thick Fife or Lothians accent. He would stomp into the castle, dashing his hand through thinning tousled hair and wheezing a little. 'Aye, well, let's hae a look then.' We would climb up to the rooms with the painted ceilings, Rab usually in front, taking two steps at a time despite his wee legs, and a little breathless. 'Look there,' he said, his stubby fingers jabbing at the ceiling. 'It's about time for another go, I think.' One small room had bits of fresco peeping out from the later emulsion. 'These will just have tae wait till we have a better idea how tae get yon paint off.' I was gung-ho for getting stuck in. 'Naw, naw,' he would say. 'There's plenty easier bits tae be getting on with.' So we stuck to sticking the flakes back on to the ceilings.

Rab had known Schomberg Scott, the architect for the repairs after the fire. We stood looking at the tiny remnants of fresco over the High Hall windows. He sniffed, rocking on his feet with restrained energy, and drew his hand through his hair in a gesture of determined bustle. 'Schomberg thought he could see bits of colour on that wa',' he said, pointing at the plaster on the gable. 'He thought it must have been a huge royal coat of arms.' In the next room he pointed at a round boss in the middle

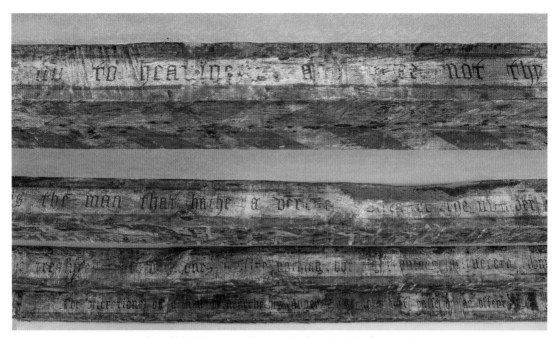

The old bathroom ceiling in Crathes Castle after repair

of the ceiling. 'That was covered in gold and the ceiling around was blue with a constellation of stars around it.' We decided that these should be left until a later time to find.

Together we had hoped to find a way to slow down the rate at which the Crathes ceilings were flaking, because every few years the Stenhouse staff would return and carefully stick the flakes back to the timber joists before they could float down to the floor. The solution seemed to be to control the environment. Many attempts were made to find a safe way to achieve this but none have been successful. The most complex proposal arose following a lecture tour I did in America in 1993.

I found myself in the Union League Club in leafy, waspish Pennsylvania, where I spoke to a large group of members in a room where the walls were decorated with images from the *Song of Solomon*, rather rude and therefore unexpected. A balding and bespectacled English environmental control specialist was there too with lots of images of Oxford and successful installations he had made with air conditioning and the like. On his return he came to visit and tried to offer a solution. One idea was to insert air conditioning plant into the chimney.

Rab and I thought long and hard about this. He rocked back and forth on his heels, sucked his teeth and stared quizzically up at me. So the decision was taken: no. It can be a bit too easy to turn to technology for a solution, incurring a big cost and a lot of maintenance, when what is really needed is simply to manage the place as a home with heating and simple ventilation. We would just have to continue to stick the flakes back up when they appeared.

Crathes Castle ceilings and their conservation

Rab remained with the centre until he retired, when he began to paint for his own amusement and exhibition. He spent his career working with the decorative and figurative images of the past but in retirement returned to his first love as an abstract artist. Sometimes he would stay with me on his visits and, usually with a large dram in his hand, he would speak of the famed Scottish artist John Bellany, whom he greatly admired. 'We were at art school around the same time. Great man and there's nobody that could hold a candle tae him, except maybe Alan Davie.' Rab lived a colourful life and died in 2013. Another character had moved on.

13
TWO HILLS

'Hello, it's Bill,' said the voice on the phone. 'Which one?' I wondered. There were quite a few around the Trust at the time. It was 2004. This one was Professor Bill Hamilton, who had been a regular delegate at our conservation conferences in the 1990s and in his early life had worked at MacFarlane & Co., an iron foundry in Glasgow. We had maintained a correspondence over the years and he now wanted me to address the annual meeting of the Institute of Surveyors in Malaysia where he now led the surveying course at his new university. The invitation to speak was, frankly, too good an opportunity to miss, though embarrassment would inevitably ensue, as so often seems to be the case in my experience.

So in summer the following year I found myself stepping out of a stunning new airport in Kuala Lumpur into a wall of humidity—something that has to be experienced to be believed. Bill then took me to his car and off we sped to his flat just outside the city.

An hour or so later I sat on the balcony of his apartment after a journey passing palm oil plantations and then listening to the tropical birds and insects as Bill prepared some green tea. I recall thinking of an old neighbour from my childhood who lived up the stairs from me in the Glasgow tenement we shared. He had been a prisoner on the Burma railway, and I wondered how anyone could have lived through the experience in that heat and humidity. He was a large, bespectacled man with a friendly disposition, especially towards us children. When he was released in 1945 he had to be carried from the PoW camp, having lost around two-thirds of his bodyweight. He died, childless, many years ago and speaking about him to my hosts over the next few days I heard many similar and worse stories from the native Malays. I mention him now as his story is probably forgotten by all but me.

So many interesting things begin with an innocuous phone call and so it had been a few years earlier in 2001 when the slightly high-pitched, rather posh voice of a kindly benefactor came through on a crackly line. He lives in the remote west, where telephone connections still seemed to be a novelty. 'Hellooo,' he said with rising excitement. 'Have you seen that Craigievar hill is for sale?' Even away in the west he had an insight and contacts that defeated most.

Hans Coper vase

Craigievar hill

'No,' I said, 'but if you are over why not have a look?'

When we managed to meet at the castle months later it was mid-week on a dull, overcast day and, as we strode up a track at the side of a field filled with yowes (ewes), the heavens opened. The rain began to fall as it sometimes does in Aberdeenshire. This is not a fine highland mist that might appear romantic and windswept from the window of a comfortable croft; it is a downpour, and where once there were long views to low hills there was now little to be seen but blackish-grey sheets of water hammering the ground. Within minutes the sheep looked like old Labradors after an unwelcome bath.

The well-spoken islander was not to be put off. Wind and rain were hardly novelties in the land of the Gael, and in our inappropriate footwear and with limited weatherproof clothing we set off, slipping and stumbling through the woodland and fields to the top and back down the other side. Curiously, I had a small umbrella with me and anyone might have laughed to have seen two men stumbling and sliding up the slippery slope through patches of Sitka spruce under a wholly inadequate and ineffectual umbrella, but that is how it went, and we completed the tour in a couple of hours.

We mulled over many things while walking on the hill as there was a long-standing problem with damp in the castle from repairs there in the 1970s, while he had been a guide, and he was concerned about parts of the collection. I was too as this was now within my remit as conservation manager, and we spoke about a small collection of

Studio pottery collected by Lady Sempill

Japanese military decorations owned by the last laird, a pioneering aviator who had been in Japan before the war and had been honoured by the emperor with the Order of the Rising Sun. The laird's second wife, Lady Cecelia, was an art dealer who championed the work of potter Bernard Leach in her London Gallery. Leach lived for a time in Japan working with the founders of the Mingei movement, which celebrated traditional crafts and in particular the work of potter Shoji Hamada and of Soetsu Yanagi, author of *The Unknown Craftsman*. This contact would have a profound influence on the taste for studio pottery in the UK and some of it would find its way to Craigievar.

I was once able to visit Kyoto and saw at first hand the stoneware that these craftspeople drew their inspiration from. It can be seen in the temples and sub-temples. In that setting they take on a different role, forming part of a holistic artistic expression encompassing gardens, architecture, flower arranging, calligraphy, clothing, movement and so on. The placing of these items in the elegance of Craigievar now seems to me a bit like an exotic creature removed from its native habitat.

Lady Cecilia's artistry on the castle, however, should not be underestimated in her aesthetic use of rush matting, white walls and the scrubbed granite stairs. Her collection of stoneware is striking and the most spectacular pot that she introduced is probably the Hans Coper vase that returned to the place as a permanent part of the collection soon after that hill walk and thanks to the islander. It now sits on the sill in the Great

Hans Coper vase in its perspex box

Hall, encased, to my disappointment, in a perspex box. The vase is monumental, with a spherical base and flattened cylindrical neck with brown and cream glazes. I love it.

I might not love the perspex, but it saved us from disaster.

During the major repairs to resolve the damp in the building in 2008, the castle was encased in scaffolding and the windows were boarded to prevent damage. All of the collections had been packed, but the vase was safe in its box and left on the sill.

Towards the end of the repairs the windows were being repainted and the protective boards that covered them through the builder work were removed one by one and then replaced immediately after the painting was done. At lunchtime one day, as the workers made their way down to the sheds, a small pebble was dislodged from the scaffolding above. It fell until it was just above the Great Hall, where it hit a scaffolding pole and ricocheted into the window, creating a neat bullet-like hole. Its trajectory took it to the perspex box, where it harmlessly bounced off, leaving the vase unchipped. Later that day I stood in the hall with the site foreman. We puffed out our cheeks at the lucky escape and got the window fixed.

As the benefactor and I returned from our wet walk up the hill, I should have reported to Daphne the manager, who I knew would soon have the kettle on and cake on the table, with her cats swirling around our legs. Today, though, there would be no cake.

I got to the castle, soaked and freezing, to find the new CEO and his wife on a surprise visit. I stood dripping onto the stair and told him of my expedition. The benefactor had seen him and quickly disappeared. The large and avuncular CEO had recently arrived at the Trust from a life in wildlife conservation and, curiously, at a time when the Trust chairman was also director of Edinburgh Zoo.

Some said it was a unique experience to have two elephant experts running the Trust. Well, elephants were far from our minds unless the hill was to be a white one, so we had a quick review of a possible acquisitions appraisal as we stood on the stair outside the Great Hall. We agreed it looked like something worthwhile, but only if donors could be found. A fundraising campaign was required and the tweedy and lugubrious head of fundraising led the challenge.

The campaign was successful and within a few days the asking price for the hill was achieved with a little extra to support conservation work. I spoke to the lawyers and an offer was made and accepted and the hill is now a firm part of the visitor experience to

Craigievar. School parties come there looking for fungi and rabbit droppings with the ranger service, which had created tours and trails, and it has turned out to be a great success.

I had had another, rather wet stroll up a hill, this time with Prof. Bill in the damp air of Malaysia, not in Japan, sadly. There was no rain but I was bent over by the aftermath of an unfortunate culinary experience and the highest levels of humidity you could imagine.

I had given my address to the Malaysian Institute of Surveyors in Kuala Lumpur and wee Bill arranged for me to meet the director of the National Museum of Malaysia and his senior team, but the night before the big meeting I found myself in a tricky position. I had set off into the centre of Kualua Lumpur alone. If only Bill had been there, I thought later.

I enjoyed a fine meal in the centre of town near the Petronas Towers, beside spectacular fountains that sent huge quantities of water into the air, but I got lost on the way home and found myself in a strange part of town when from the other side of the road came an odd sound. 'Coo-yee!'

'Hmmm,' I thought, 'What's this?'

From the corner of my eye I could see a small group of ladies, one of whom set off, clacking in high-heeled shoes towards me. I strode on with increased determination and purpose but this was to no avail and soon a small hand grabbed my elbow. As I turned around with the word 'No' forming on my lips, my eye travelled up from the scuffed white stilettos past the minuscule attire to the face, which was adorned with a moustache. I drew on all my Glaswegian confidence and smiled, 'No thank you,' and strode on, to catcalls and whistles.

I woke the next morning with the unmistakable stomach cramps of food poisoning. The heat and the food had got me. Soon I was in a car on my way to the museum, and Bill and I walked through the humidity, climbing up to the top of the building. I could feel my head droop, beads of sweat appeared and my hands began to tremble. I creased with embarrassment as the staff cast sideways glances at the shambling, sweaty figure walking carefully through the office.

Within minutes I was in the director's suite, squirming and trying to focus. The door opened, the unmistakable clink of the tea trolley arrived and a faint aroma of coffee filled the room. My heart sank as they brought out sandwiches and my stomach twisted, accompanied by a small squeak of discomfort. I tried not to pay attention as coffee was poured and then, to my increasing anguish, sweetened condensed milk was poured into it. The sweet caffeine aroma met my nose and my vision blurred. My hands tightened on the arms of the chair and I could take no more, so before I completely disgraced myself I stood with as much grace as I could manage, made my apologies and stumbled away with a determined expression on my face. I was found a little later flat out on a bench just outside the building. The kindly director took a little pity on me, and Bill and I were driven to Malacca the next day in his chauffeured car.

We sat in comfort in the large 4x4 as we sped south along the Malacca straits. When we arrived we were met by the local manager of the museum service. The national

Craigievar hill woodland trail

director was determined to look after us very well and arranged for this honour. The small man marched us through the colonial centre of the town until we reached the low hill with the ruined St Paul's church perched on top. Still a bit shaky, I felt my legs wobble in anticipation of the very short climb.

We passed architectural remnants of colonial rulers, from the Portuguese to the Dutch and finally the British buildings, many of them painted a startling red in imitation of the colour the British seemed to favour.

Bill and I later made our way to the Chinese area of town, which was thronged with traders and tourists. The Chinese were everywhere; though China never controlled Malaysia its diaspora is very obvious. Bill and I navigated the broken pavements and shop-houses looking for somewhere to rest. Many of the older shops are built in a Chinese courtyard style and finding one we stumbled into a set of rooms crowded around a small garden courtyard where the sun was filtered through wrought iron and the doors are placed to cause a gentle draught. We sat at a tiny round iron table and pots of oolong were set by us as we prepared for the next exertion. Eventually I felt my stomach settle and my legs stop shaking from climbing the little hill to St Paul's church.

We got back to Kuala Lumpur and soon got into a bus and set off north, passing endless palm oil plantations in thick tropical heat to the island of Penang and to the Blue Mansion in George Town, once the home of Cheong Fatt Tze, a twentieth century shipping and industrial magnate. Stepping into the cool of the interior, though there was no air conditioning, Bill smiled with a proprietorial air at iron columns holding up iron fretted balconies and staircases, all from his old workplace foundry in Glasgow.

The mansion was built to Feng Shui principles and in consequence sits askew to the street front. Within, the complex the rooms are placed around several roofless courtyards and the main one has a sunken floor where we were sitting late that evening when a tropical storm struck. The stars disappeared from overhead and silver streams of rain fell into a pond forming in that reservoir. There was a gurgle and whoosh as the rain from the massive roof was channelled through Glaswegian cast iron ducts, shooting out at force into the pool, a temporary display of cascading water to cool the residents.

The Penang Heritage Trust had saved the mansion from demolition and also championed the old commercial trades that operated within the tightly clustered houses nearby. Next day the heat and humidity returned and we set off through the town following the Trust's trail and into a shop-house where the front room held the cluttered accoutrements of a poor Chinese family alongside dozens of bags of coffee beans. It was a coffee roasting factory and in the back room ancient

Penang Heritage Trust leaflets (IMD)

machinery roasted the beans and prepared them for use. Passing through this pungent house and around a corner to the next street, we found slipper makers fashioning colourful embroidered footwear. Another house in the neighbourhood had been turned into a jewellery store where behind a tiny counter the proprietor would offer trays of heavy gold jewellery and nearby, sitting on the floor, an elderly Indian would fashion the items before you. Yet another house front sat open and was stacked with boxes of incense sticks, made in the back room and sold by a tiny withered elderly man to the Hindu temples, which were undoubtedly the most exotic of places, festooned with deities' flowers and petals and a detritus of worship that included a wave of sickly odour. Like Dorothy, I was not in Kansas anymore.

Too soon I was back in Scotland and my new role as interim regional director, after my predecessor had moved 'upstairs' to run concerts and big events. He was a besuited, commercial chap who had let me get on with the conservation side of the business. Now I returned from Malaysia ready to lead the region for a while and eventually to tackle that damp at Craigievar.

14

AN ESTATE IN RUINS

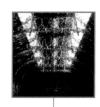

One winter afternoon I fell out of the window of Derry Lodge, deep in the Cairngorms. The window was on the ground floor so no damage was done. Looking up, I saw a herd of antlered stags a few metres away who glanced with quiet indifference and continued to nuzzle at food left for them by the staff on Mar Lodge Estate. This was 1996, and my assistant surveyor, D.K., was less keen on big fauna than I was, so we got into the Land Rover and edged away down the track and back to the big house, Mar Lodge itself.

I had climbed in through the window earlier in the day because Derry Lodge was derelict and had been boarded up and the window was easier to open than the door, but as I clambered in my usual ungainly manner onto the sill and pulled my knee up to my chin, my foot slipped on the wet timber and I tumbled out.

A few weeks earlier, there had been a meeting of the estate management committee. 'What is to be done with Derry?' asked the plummy voice of the chairman at the head of the table. Everyone who tramped through the hills seemed to have an opinion, and after the Trust arrived people expected action.

Poor old Derry was not in good shape. There were huge holes in the roof and floors had been ripped up by walkers to make campfires.

D.K. and I arrived for this trip to the glen together, entering the estate where the cast iron bridge crosses the river, and we drove on up to the office in the stables. The hill behind it appeared to be covered with tombstones where the stumps of trees cut down by Canadian loggers decades before were slowly rotting into the ground among heather that was cropped by the hundreds of deer. No new tree would dare poke its head up for fear of a nibble.

Our Land Rover bounced and pitched along rough tracks up to Derry Lodge, where we stepped carefully through litter and human faeces before clambering in through the window to stand in the musty gloom and the debris. It seemed a sad end for a rather dignified house.

Our torches illuminated the dust motes as light seeped through the cracks at the edges of the boarded windows. Old plaster crunched underfoot and when we climbed the stair we realised that the floor was rotted from a huge hole in the roof. The walkers

The stag ballroom, Mar Lodge

Mar Lodge

Derry Lodge in 1994

Derry Lodge, late 19th century

who had broken in had smashed through walls to crawl from room to room. D.K. muttered quietly as we stumbled round.

That trip to Derry was not my first foray to the estate. That had happened about two years earlier when the new management committee were thinking of a possible future for the big hoose. Some thought it should be subdivided into holiday apartments and the committee agreed. The plummy chairman asked me, 'Is this something you could do?' The Grampian director, my manager at the time, was not keen; he could see the support for his properties diminishing, especially as he had very few staff, just a factor, a public relations officer and a couple of secretaries besides D.K. and me.

That director was a dashing and handsome chap, straight out of a Jilly Cooper novel, with windswept, longish, sun-bleached hair, and when he spoke, his striking blue eyes held you and he could charm any audience. There was never any doubt that he had arrived, entering every room with a flourish, a bird of paradise fluttering and flashing his colourful feathers.

Despite his concerns, I stayed on secondment to the estate, working two, sometimes five days a week there, and I escaped back to Grampian with a sense of relief when it ended in 1996. It had been such a challenging time that, on what should have been my last visit, I stopped the car as I left the estate and got out to stamp off the dust of the place from my feet. However, I was to find myself back there in 2000, for another challenging, but this time happier period.

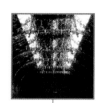

In the stables on that first visit, the factor was sitting in a rather bare office. He looked up with a beaming smile, his head crowned with thick black wiry hair. He reminded me a little of a diminutive Omar Sharif in a waxed jacket. Over at the big house, the housekeeper Mrs Dempster and her enthusiastic terrier waited. 'Oh, yes. Yes, aye,' she would say in a high-pitched voice when anyone asked for help. She showed me into the stag ballroom to see the hundreds of skulls that festooned the walls and ceilings in gruesome array, the dagger-like points of the antlers aimed at my head. I had never thought to see anything like this, especially when green lights were lit under them and the black holes of their eye sockets remained in shadow.

The next person I met at Mar Lodge was Peter the ranger, who had just arrived on the estate and needed a home, so the factor pointed out a house at the end of the track that loops behind the big lodge—a plain, late eighteenth century two-storey building unused for about twenty years.

I took the Historic Scotland inspector up to have a look, to get his views on assisting us through the legislative labyrinth. We crunched over broken plaster, stepping on

The stag ballroom, Mar Lodge

broken glass, and stood in rooms last decorated in the 1970s. The peeling wallpapers were inexpensive, with bold patterns of large, stylised brown and yellow flowers on a cream background. This had been a brave choice for the decorator even then.

The inspector pondered tongue in cheek if this would have to be conserved. 'I lived through the 1970s. I didn't like this then, and I still don't!'

The Trust's intention for the estate was to combine the Highland sporting estate activities with nature conservation, two ethoses that had seemed incompatible. 'If there are enough ptarmigan,' the sports shooters would state, 'we should shoot them. They're game birds after all, don't you know.' The mountain walkers would then turn white and fall over. 'Bunny huggers,' the tweedy hunters would mutter ominously.

The winds of change had arrived and the whole Trust was beginning to morph into something new and more commercial, with a greater role for members in an enhanced committee structure. The Trust had always had advisory committees to assist staff, but the glaring omission from the list was the committee for buildings, which was now to be formed of representatives from the architectural profession and others. The buildings committee was led by Charles McKean, an architectural historian of some note and a contrarian as a hobby.

Charles was like an intellectual Roman candle and when asked about any architectural topic would explode with a cascade of novel imaginative thoughts that were always illuminating and entertaining. He had the knack of making everyone seem as clever as he was himself. Sadly, Charles died in 2013.

He took his committee members around the estate just after the buildings committee had been formed. Around the same time, another visitor was the director of the Centre for Conservation at York University. Peter Burman would later go on to be the Trust's director of conservation, though neither of us knew this at the time. He and I had a shared interest in the scattered ruins on Mar Lodge Estate as we were both involved with the Society for the Protection of Ancient Buildings, Peter in a position that reflected his status and me as a Scottish committee member.

Both Charles and Peter wanted to see the ruins, and their reactions to Derry were remarkably similar. 'Oh, my, how marvellous!' 'Gosh, isn't it something?'

Peter Burman MBE (Peter Burman)

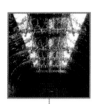

The Red House, Mar Lodge (IMD)

'Something should be done... what?' 'Hmmm,' then silence.

After Derry they went to see another ruin, the Red House. From a distance it seemed delightful with a rusty red iron roof over a symmetrical facade and two windows and a door. The shallow river beside us was low and the round boulders could be seen at the ford that took you further inland. Getting closer, you realise that the windows and door are black holes and the chimney looks drunken. There were huge cracks and a massive collapse in the gable wall. Inside, the floor was festooned with the debris of a thousand campers and when it was cleaned out, deep in the debris a set of false teeth was discovered.

Standing there with Charles and his committee, and later with Peter, it looked as if the defects were not so bad and that the Red House could be easily saved. The management committee, however, wanted it removed because the vandalism and defects made it a hazard.

The two committees disagreed and so decided to have all of the ruins inspected and their future agreed before any final decision was made. 'Ian,' they said, 'off you go and we need a report for the next meeting.'

'Good grief,' I thought. 'Do they know what they are asking?' The estate is littered with hundreds of ruins, and I feared I would never deliver this report. In desperation I asked, 'When is a ruin not a ruin?' The answer I offered them was, 'When it's a dilapidated building.' The point I was trying to make was that a ruin would be conserved as a ruin and should look pretty much unchanged, but a dilapidated building could have a future use. The Red House was to fall into the latter category.

Everyone agreed that, if a structure was unused but still roofed and the damage was neglect rather than a conscious decision or significant event, then it was dilapidated and capable of reinstatement. They also agreed that the Trust should intervene with a ruin only if it presented a health and safety hazard. Each building was assessed in turn and when the initial inspections were complete the estate committee had a ninety-page report including thoughts on the Red House. As I described my recommendations I could feel the temperature rising.

The report's conclusion was that the Red House should be consolidated, but this advice was not accepted. The estate committee reiterated their view that it be demolished, to the consternation of the buildings committee. I was now in the middle of the wild land debate, where there was a view that signs of human activity should be removed wherever possible.

It was made more interesting when Historic Scotland visited in their capacity as guardians of ancient monuments and determined that the site around the Red House be scheduled, thereby stopping the demolition. You could watch from a safe distance as choleric committee men turned purple with suppressed rage.

A less challenging place than the Red House was Bynack Lodge, a roofless tumbled ruin that had been occupied just in living memory. The last resident was now an elderly

Bynack Lodge, Mar Lodge in 1994

Bynack Lodge, Mar Lodge in 1994

lady, living in Ballater, who could recall developing appendicitis as a young girl while living there. Her journey to receive medical help took two days and required her to travel first by pony across the river ford to the roadside a few miles further up the track, then by carriage to the rail station in Ballater to await a train into Aberdeen.

A group stood at Bynack Lodge one sunny day among some of the last ancient pine trees, including the property manager and some other countryside experts, and I noticed that they all had a curious verbal tic.

Suddenly one would exclaim 'Pipit!' or some other small bird's name. They would all nod in agreement and I would look on, bemused, seeing nothing. However, on that day in the Cairngorms one of them pointed to the sky as a sea eagle flew overhead. They were amazed, we were about as far as you can get from the sea in Scotland and even I could see it.

'How can you tell it's a sea eagle?'

'Well,' we were informed sagely, 'if you hear someone say, "That's a big bird," then it's a buzzard, and if they say "That's a *really* big bird," it's a golden eagle, but if they say, "Good grief, look at the size of that!" then it's a sea eagle.'

There was a general nodding of heads.

15

THE RUDE SPOUT OF CRAIGIEVAR

I was looking up at the Sheela na gig water spout on Craigievar Castle with Neal Sharp in 1996. It is a figurative carving of a naked woman displaying her nether regions in the most graphic manner. Such carvings are said to ward off death and evil; some of them highlight another nearby orifice.

This rude spout was set above the castle door ready to soak visitors, but it had long been disused and although this prosaic function was lost, its supernatural endeavours continued and evil was usually averted. Neal and I did not dwell on this. We were there because I had hatched a plan to sort out a problem with damp in the building and I wanted Neal's thoughts about replacing the harl with traditional lime, rather than the cement that was there at the time. Neal was on his final visit, as he was due to retire as head of buildings.

He was a short, sharp-featured man, with an uncanny resemblance to Kenneth Williams, the *Carry On* movie actor and raconteur. I would visit his office in the basement of a tall tenement in Charlotte Square in Edinburgh, which was shared by many other Trust staff, ranging from the director of finance in the attic to the gardens team in the middle. He would announce his arrival each morning with a loud 'Halloooo' before taking up residence behind his desk.

Neal had many mannerisms and as we sat on the ancient hard seats in the Craigievar manager's office he took a deep sniff, flared his nostrils as he usually did at the start of a monologue, and threw his head back, remembering L.G. of Inverurie, the tradesman who reharled the castle in 1973. 'Oh yes,' he sighed, 'the castle was beautiful when we finished... golden in the sunshine. Did you know L.G. also harled Leith Hall?'

Gargoyle water spout over the entrance to Craigievar Castle (IMD)

Craigievar Castle, south elevation

'Yes,' I replied, 'and I knew his father,' also called L.G.

Old L.G. sometimes appeared in the pub I frequented following pipe band practice, a hobby long since abandoned. Sandy, the local architect, told me a little about him.

L.G. was a well-known character in Inverurie and in his later years often inebriated. The door of the Banks of Ury would creak open and old L.G. would limp in, wearing a battered Homburg hat and greatcoat, not unlike Max Wall the music hall star. He may have had an artificial leg, but his limp was not always due to the prosthetic. Sometimes he would recognise me and I would be regaled with rude stories of the building trade, too ribald for these pages.

Sandy was wary of him with good reason. At Hogmanay he would visit his house, fu' as usual. After a while he would become enraged and chase Sandy around the sofa until he could be removed. Old L.G. is long gone now, as is his son.

Removing the old stair roof, 1973 – Neal Sharp holds the ladder

The Pepperpot being taken away

Trust joiner Johnnie Morgan making the new turret roof

The Pepperpots being lifted back into place

I had not had much to do with Neal till he took over the role of head of buildings in 1993. He became a Trust surveyor in the early 1960s, based in Inverness and at Balmacara on the west coast. 'How you must have loved it,' I said, trying to draw out a recollection from him.

'One of the unhappiest times of my life,' he told me during the retirement party I had unwittingly arranged for him there.

I had heard about Neal first from Johnnie Morgan, the joiner I managed. They had worked together and liked each other and they created ogee roofs for the pavilions in the walled garden at Pitmedden and the small roofs over the turnpike stairs at Craigievar. Johnnie loved that sort of challenge and Neal was just the chap to make it happen.

Neal was not someone who took kindly to being managed and in particular he seemed to rail against architects. His relationship with the consultant architect from the 1960s and 70s, Schomberg Scott, was a little frosty. 'The bugger never visited,' he would say when remembering jobs they were involved with. 'I had to do it all by myself,' but that was how he liked it. Pointing at the public toilets at Craigievar car park he would say, in parody of the Latin inscription on Sir Christopher Wren's grave in St Paul's Cathedral, 'If you seek my monument, look around you.'

His great love was the Little Houses Improvement Scheme, a building preservation project administered by the Trust that acquires and restores smaller houses and which was largely responsible for the preservation of townscapes at Culross and Dunkeld and in the East Neuk of Fife, along with many other triumphs elsewhere. He worked there with Judith, a statuesque woman with long pre-Raphaelite hair, who delivered the projects for him. I am sure she appears in paintings by Rossetti, wandering through a verdant glade, her flame-coloured hair glinting in the sun.

As Neal and I stood at the foot of Craigievar and looked up at the bendy lady high up on the walls, we could see disused waterspouts and decorative cannons all around the corbelling under the roof. There were lots of gaps where some had been knocked off, with about half of the cannons gone and most of the spouts too.

The remaining cannons have many different shapes. Some are cylindrical and others polygonal with decoration on the underside to be viewed from the ground. Looking up, though, you need good eyesight to make out the detail in the stone so far away. I suspect they might once have been painted in a glorious Technicolor, though I have never found any evidence for that. I like to think that Craigievar would have been very bright and maybe even startling to our eyes and that the impression we have of dull, dour, forbidding fortified houses is a recent phenomenon.

The taste for dull and subdued colours is curious. I remember once speaking to a conservator from the Sistine chapel, who on revealing the vibrancy under the centuries of incense smoke, was criticised by some historians who said when it was pointed out that these were Michelangelo's colours, 'Well, he got it wrong.'

The most intricate of Craigievar's carvings are over the only door. These would have been visible from within the walled courtyard and the last remnant of this wall, known as the barmkin, is now a wildflower rockery in summer. If you had arrived in past centuries in this enclosed space you would have been faced with a vertical grouping on the castle walls of an iron-studded oak door with a carved armorial above set beneath double storey turrets around a balustrade-enclosed platform and topped with a gilded weathercock—an imposing monumental impression on an otherwise small tower.

Neal told me on that visit that Scott Sutherland, the architect who gave his name to the school of architecture in Aberdeen, would roar up to the castle on his motorbike in the 1950s, despite having lost a leg, and would climb up to this platform only to hop on his remaining leg around the parapet.

Craigievar as you see it today was not the first tower on this site. The original home of the Mortimers of Craigievar, who had owned the estate since the late 1300s, was remodelled in the early seventeenth century when the ornate roofline was created and the interior radically altered by 'Danzig Willie' Forbes. Willie, whose thug-like portrait hangs in the castle, was the younger son of a local laird and a merchant to the Baltic ports, who would use his wealth to great effect.

Today, as you ascend the larger of two turnpike stairs, you find rooms created for comfortable living, not rough lodgings. The Long Gallery at the top, the largest room in the castle, would have been bright and comfortable with large windows looking east

Looking up to the parapet

over the Strath and round turrets in each corner where many small windows gave a panoramic view. There are doors that take you to stairways rising to viewing platforms, each set behind granite balustrades.

Danzig Willie decided to reform the old tower to create his home rather than replace it. He could have had an imposing house in the fashionable long and low style favoured at Drum Castle nearby or at the great palace at Huntly, each remodelled around the same time. Why, I have wondered, did Willie decide against this? Some have suggested it was for defensive purposes. He lived in challenging times and the covenanting wars were to rage nearby only thirty years later, but I feel that was not the determining factor in the design of his home. Others with greater insight than me are better placed to provide an answer.

I have been responsible for the wellbeing of Craigievar and other similar places for over thirty years and as I reflect on the experience I see Craigievar as unique in its conception and its development. Other houses may be older, larger and richer, but Craigievar seems to epitomise a curiously restrained elegance that grows out of an older tradition. It reflects more dangerous or perhaps less settled times by refining the memes, or cultural traditions, of the ancient district of Mar to create an idiosyncratic, asymmetrical, vertical sculpture. The plain harled walls rise four storeys with rounded corners and lean inwards from the ground to the corbel to give an illusion of slenderness to an otherwise dumpy building, topped with decoration and complex roof structures that further emphasise the verticality.

The decorative stonework is, in the most part, carved from forgiving yellow sandstone while some carvings are created from the rough red local granite. This is not a fine-grained material; it is roughly textured igneous rock with large crystals of feldspar in which it is almost impossible to create fine detail, especially when working with soft iron tools three hundred and fifty years ago.

I took Neal up to Craigievar for his last visit not so much to view the decoration or the scatological lady, or even to recount his stories, but to get his support.

The journey that led to this visit had begun long before, when I had become worried while examining cracks on the ceilings in 1983 and had set out to prove the problem was caused by the harl, made with cement, and also by an increase in the popularity of the castle, where visitor numbers had tripled in ten years with thousands of tramping feet marching over the fragile floors.

I did not make the connection between the harl and the cracks at first, until it was pointed out to me by Dr Chris George, a timber decay specialist from London whom I had met when he was working on Brighton Pavilion. Chris came to Craigievar to determine if the woodworm in the castle was a problem for us. As we toured the castle I told him about the cracks and the near collapse of a turret ceiling. We got up onto the viewing platform on the roof and peered around. Chris suddenly pointed at the turret with the ceiling and said, 'There is your problem... there.' The harling had washed off in the rain where the wall bulged slightly.

I realised that the Craigievar cracks were caused by two things. The first was damp from the cement harl and the second was the sheer number of visitors. The ceilings needed to be repaired and then protected by reducing the effect of visitors' feet and the cement harl would have to go and be replaced with lime that would allow the place to dry.

Everything takes time and sometimes it seems to take the length of a career to get things done. So it was with the cement harl.

I bored everyone to death speaking about this and faces would glaze over whenever the subject came up. Throughout the 1980s and 90s, I set out to gather evidence to persuade everyone that the cement in the harl was the issue. I even undertook a post-graduate diploma where my dissertation was entitled *Harling—History, Development and Use*, and authored a Trust booklet about harling, which must have been the slowest selling publication in Trust history.

There was some effect though, and I found myself working informally with Historic Scotland and amenity societies, where I was called on to speak at conferences around the country, proselytising the use of lime, the traditional material. So it was that I found myself at the University of York. I appeared at the King's Manor near Petergate with a cartridge of slide images under my arm and a silly grin on my face to deliver a forty-minute lecture on harling, a subject with limited appeal, one might think. Peter, the course leader, introduced me to the crowd of mature students. 'Ian will be with you for the next hour and a half and I will be back at lunchtime.'

An hour and a half! 'Extemporise slowly,' I thought and remembered how I had managed to get the attention of the Women's Rural Institute meeting I had spoken to and tried to weave in tales of ghosts. Peter returned to find me perched on the desk imitating the man destined soon to be a ghost at Craigievar being forced out of the window at sword point. It can't have been too bad. I was invited back.

Every time I am in York, I visit the west front of the Minster to say hello. That is where, in 1996, I met the Cirencester-based sculptor Rory Young, the designer and carver of the sixteen panels of the Genesis cycle on the great west door of York Minster, and I took the experience back with me to Craigievar thinking of those missing cannons. Perhaps, I thought, I could have them replaced.

Time went by and in 1999 I was asked to become the deputy director and conservation manager for the new North East region and to pull together a conservation team with staff to support everything from archaeology to collections, education to forestry and everything else in between. The issues at Craigievar would be parked for a while.

The team was assembled over about a year and among them were two surveyors. Dave Chouman arrived first, an architect from Aberdeen. Then came Gavin McCall, a big man in terms of his height, his abilities and his standards. He became the champion for the repair of Craigievar. Dave and Gavin now manage their own businesses, having moved on from the Trust in 2007.

The office was filled with new faces and we built our team with games, paper aeroplane competitions and cake-making forfeits for meetings. Slowly a network of supporters grew until one day a message came through that I had a visitor at the reception desk. I knew this chap, so through he came.

The door swung open and this tall man in a woolly jumper, burdened with carrier bags filled with papers took a seat. Stretching out his long legs, he smoothed his bushy beard. He rummaged in one of the bags and produced my wee booklet on harling. 'I was just re-reading this little booklet of yours,' he said in a slightly high-pitched, rather posh voice. 'Do you still think Craigievar should be reharled?'

'Yes,' I said without any hesitation. 'Well,' he said, 'let's do it,' and his financial support and enthusiasm allowed the whole project to move forward.

That was around 2004. I asked Gavin to be the Trust project manager, and his attention to detail and calm assertive nature soon had everyone together. Even the Royal Commission on the Ancient and Historical Monuments of Scotland offered their artist, John Borland, to draw the many carved and decorative stones on the tower. John would spend many hours on the scaffolding creating such wonderful images that he and I were able to publish another slow-selling booklet, *Gargoyles and Water Spouts*, at the end of the project.

But in 2004 that publication was still a long way off and there were many trips and slips to be avoided before the repairs could happen. As a local worthy said to me at the time, 'The bite's nae yours till it's in your mou.' In other words, don't count your chickens. The worthy in question was the farmer, author and raconteur Charlie Allan, who sang at the retirement party for the Trust joiner Johnnie Morgan.

As for the rude spout, she is now on display in the castle. We could not reaffix her without damage, and it is much easier to view her on a table top. I had her laid out in the Long Gallery with her head furthest away and her 'bottom' nearest the viewer. She smiles maniacally from a disc-like face with her ankles behind her ears and hands grasping and displaying her... let's just say 'herself'.

I am not sure everyone appreciates the view and she is often turned around to protect her modesty. I suspect she is outraged when this happens, and I return her to a more explicit revelation.

John Borland of the RCAHMS

125

16
TRUE GRIT

I was pleased that I didn't have the team around me when Craigievar was wreathed in plumes of dust as a grit blaster attacked the cement on the castle walls in the summer of 2009. There are times you need to be alone with your thoughts. Conservation is all about gathering evidence and making sound decisions based on analysis. It is a team exercise, but when you are faced with racket and dirt on a much-loved ancient building there can sometimes be too many opinions. I imagined the most sensitive of my team, heads in their hands, perhaps even tears streaking their grit-covered faces.

If there is one activity I never expected to do on a Trust building, it was grit blasting, particularly after my experiences on tenements in Glasgow in 1982, which I have regretted ever since.

The blasting team's van was parked at the castle door and the generator roared with a din I am sure has never before been experienced on the hill. That day I parked as usual at the manager's cottage, whose doors and windows were firmly shut against the cacophony, before setting off down the short slope to the gate in the old barmkin wall. The laburnum was in flower, drooping over rhododendrons that usually frame my favourite image of the place. I stood beside the van and watched the man with the blaster hose and my mind went back to Glasgow a few months after I had emerged from college to an office in St Enoch Square, opposite the curious Victorian ticket office to the subway.

It was here as a new graduate that I anxiously climbed up the stone stairs in an Edwardian sandstone office block, passing varnished brown doors with yellowing paint peeling from the high walls and dusty cables snaking around them. There was a curious yellow glow to the lights that gave the place a nicotine colour. I could have used the rickety iron lift in the stairwell, which had a creaky concertina door and even creakier winding gear, but I was not brave enough.

My employer soon had me working on the tenements in the south side of the city, spending the council's building repair grants. The property managers, or factors as they were usually known, had just set up a small team of surveyors to service this demand and I was part of it.

Adam Gordon carving affronted unicorns (McCall Surveying)

The factors were long established in the city, and their original role had been to extract the rent from tenants on behalf of landlords. As a child of the tenements myself, I can remember stories of wifies hiding from the factor if their man had drunk his wages that week.

The more terrifying of the Glaswegian wifies had a reputation that could send a shiver through many a rent collector. My old Dad used to joke he would throw his bunnet into the house on pay day and if it didn't get thrown back he would go in. I suspect this may not be an entirely accurate account of my parents' relationship.

The office up in that Edwardian building was occupied by gallus wee men in wide-lapelled suits with kipper ties that were notable for their extreme breadth and garish colours and patterns, and by slightly overweight ladies squeezed into tight, often sparkly, clothing, a sartorial hangover from the 1970s and their prime. To be 'gallus' is a demeanour peculiar to Glasgow that suggests cheek, self-assurance and boldness, usually accompanied by a swagger and a fondness for dressing up in ostentatiously smart clothing. They would romp through the place cracking jokes that were usually stories of the clients or their weekend fun.

Perhaps of greater interest to this young surveyor was a typing pool of glamorous young women who trailed perfume and banter, effortlessly emasculating the insolent. They were led by a terrifying wee wummin called Agnes—or Senga, as Diana, the petite, feisty blonde and the youngest of them, called her. Diana would put me in my place for some minor misdemeanour while perched on the edge of the desk and fixing me with her bonnie blue eyes. Ah, dear reader, who would not have been happily contrite?

The new surveyors were such an exotic phenomenon in this old birdcage that we were pretty much left alone to do our worst. I usually had thirty projects running and, unlike Craigievar, I did not have the benefit of a team to help and other opinions to manage. A large part of the work was removing slates from roofs to replace them with concrete tiles, then sandblasting the soot-blackened walls to reveal the red or yellow sandstone beneath. We blasted everything and thought it a great job, but this really was not the way to care for the Victorian heritage. Grit blasting took off a layer of dirty stone

Blasting away at the cement on Craigievar in 2008
(McCall Surveying)

to leave a roughened sub-surface that was now open to the elements. We had a phrase for this as algae took hold on the rough, damp surface: clean to green in six months.

One day a factor dashed into the room I shared with three others to say that some scaffolding had collapsed in my patch. Pale and feeling alone, I hurried to the pool car, a large gold Ford Cortina that I would later buy at a knock-down price before I moved north. It rolled and swayed on loose springs through the city streets, and I rushed over the river Clyde into Pollokshaws, to a maze of rather elegant, slightly downmarket, red sandstone buildings, where I found my scaffolding was still intact, but further along the road lay another, sprawled over parked cars and unkempt gardens. This was boom time for the builders and corners were being cut. Fortunately, this time no one was hurt.

On my last day with the factors about a year later, I visited a tenement in Battlefield, part of a streetscape opposite the old Victoria Infirmary, 'the Vickie'. The street was built in the great city expansion to the south on the flood plain of the river Cart, where the buildings had sunk slowly into the alluvial mud. I wandered into the tenement opening and found massive cracks, and evidence of old attempts at propping it up. I quickly exited, reported to my manager and was glad to set out for Aberdeenshire and the National Trust for Scotland. I understand the occupants had to be moved out of that Battlefield tenement, and there was a partial collapse, but by that time I was in a small room in Pitmedden House with an old desk and a new but empty filing cabinet, wondering what I was supposed to be doing.

As I stood in front of Craigievar that dusty day, twenty-six years later, looking at the plumes of grit and remembering my hectic youth, I did not doubt that in this instance we were doing the right thing, but I was nonetheless relieved that no emotional outbursts would have to be contended with.

We knew from our research that the castle had been given a thin coating of cement and water under a dense cement harl in 1973, probably in an attempt to ensure that the new thick rough coat of mortar would stick to the old masonry below, and low-pressure grit blast was the only way to get it off.

There is a truism that it is further to travel from Edinburgh to Aberdeenshire than it is to do the opposite, meaning that Aberdonians find no challenge in going south but the reverse is not always true, and this was even more so in the early 1970s when many of the decisions on the repair of Craigievar were left to local staff, despite their limited knowledge or experience.

The 1970s cement had to come off to allow the building to dry. It was as if the place had been wrapped in polythene, trapping moisture and creating a reservoir within the walls that caused decay to the historic timbers and cracks in the ornate Jacobean plasterwork that might with little effort collapse onto the floor. It is in situations such as this that I find it helpful to realise that caring for historic buildings is a continuum, trying to 'stave off decay by daily care'[5], knowing that sometimes something bigger is needed. That was the situation at Craigievar.

There is a danger that one may consider that this big project would solve all of the problems and that once completed the building is safe in perpetuity. In my experience, the big job is only a moment of extra effort in that continuum and as much a part of staving off decay as painting the windows or cleaning the gutters, only bigger, more expensive and highly stressful to the project manager.

In taking a decision to radically change an ancient structure you really have to know how each part of the building contributes to the whole and that changing even the smallest part may impact on its significance. This needs teamwork. Gathering information, analysing it and developing policies and principles lie at the heart of projects such as this one.

Over the years, working with many colleagues, we all learned that conservation throughout the Trust should be led by an understanding of the place. Alongside me through this, but based in Glasgow, was a colleague whom I met in March 1983 when I arrived at Hutchesons' Hall to accept my new role with the Trust. Standing before me that day was a cheery round face. This was Philip Schreiber, who had been a Trust surveyor for only a few months but seemed very mature and confident, while I felt quite the opposite. 'Well, hellooo,' he said in the carefully modulated Glaswegian of the West End. Philip was not a nyaff like me.

As we grew to know each other I realised that Philip's great joy was Charles Rennie Mackintosh's Hill House in Helensburgh where he helped rediscover the missing

Holmwood House

Mackintosh decoration. Similarly, Holmwood House, designed by the curiously monikered architect Alexander 'Greek' Thomson, also had lots of hidden figurative decoration just waiting for him to find. We visited both properties together from time to time, and Philip revealed that Holmwood had latterly been part of a nunnery and that the nuns had papered and painted over the more salacious of the classical figures that Thomson had devised. Philip took great delight in having as much as possible uncovered.

He could appear a douce if cheerful wee buddy, but underneath was a committed and cheeky conservator. His great skills were quiet determination and gentle persuasion, unlike my sledgehammer approach. We had parallel careers over the next twenty-five years until his premature death in 2008.

So, when thinking about the conundrums of Craigievar, the gentle but determined attitude of Philip led me.

The castle is iconic with an aesthetic quality that is rightly celebrated. It was important to me to recognise that Craigievar is highly sculptural, using curves and shadows to create a pleasing and picturesque effect. The 1973 repairs had taken some of that away by applying a thick covering of cement. Poor old Craigievar had become chunky and the fine detailing of corners and bulges was largely lost.

Many people have noted that Craigievar has an almost organic essence, apparently growing from the hill, but as you become more aware of its shape you can see that the flat planes of walling are punctuated by windows, themselves overwhelmed by the harl, while elsewhere turnpike stairs are embedded within the walls and bulge out to create masonry cylinders that rise up to the roof.

I am drawn in particular to one corner of the roofline where there is a square turret rather than a round one, supported on a drum-like plinth whose top edge stones are exposed, giving further definition to the shape and helping rainwater to run off. Early records suggest that the red granite corbels and string courses were always visible and not covered by a coloured lime-wash. Instead the harl had been coloured to blend in with it.

The inventiveness overall is truly staggering, especially when it is remembered that this playful exterior is

Curves, planes and cannons

131

created from rough granite boulders, probably field gatherings from a few metres away. This delicate interaction of shapes and planes should be revealed to the viewer through the play of daylight and shadow. The 1973 porridge-like harl had erased much of this and I determined that a key result from our work would be to try to bring this back and that the new harl would be thin and delicate. Any opportunity to emphasise these features would be grasped.

The decision to apply a thin rather than thick harl was uncontroversial and I suspect very few people took much interest in it. Other considerations were more controversial, however, and I had to embark on lengthy negotiations to formulate policies for them.

The more contentious issues related to bits of the castle that were missing or hidden and I had to explore the realms of deep conservation philosophy to justify the decisions and ensure progress. It can be enjoyable and diverting to embark on a long, existential discussion of these matters, but it can also be expensive when you are in the middle of a complicated building project.

Some decisions could not be taken until we could see what was under the cement. Sometimes the issue was the challenging but prosaic cracks in the walls and how they should be repaired, but of greater contention was what to do about the missing decoration and more problematically what to do about the decision in 1973 to reopen blocked windows.

The castle is not an untouched survival of a seventeenth century building. Many may imply that it is, but they are wrong. The place has seen many changes and, focusing

Three of the six windows in the south-west turret

only on the exterior, there have been new windows inserted, while others have been blocked and then unblocked. There have been changes to the chimney heads, at times there have been chimney pots and at other times none, and the stairs leading to the viewing platforms now have lovely ogee lead-covered roofs, though at other times the roofs here were flat. In its earliest incarnation, the courtyard or barmkin wall would have abutted the building, but this abutment was deliberately removed in antiquity.

Craigievar is a building whose appearance has changed from time to time and usually the decision was a deliberate choice. At other times the change was accidental, for example, in the loss of much of the decoration on the roofline. Decorative water spouts and stone cannons were lost, probably when large sheets of snow slid off the slates crashing into the projections and carrying them away.

There was once a little stone man playing the bagpipes on a dormer that fell off in the 1950s. His broken remains were put on display in the building, but his face was missing. Mrs Russell, the old cleaner, told me about him around 1984. She also told me about the missing armorial panel in the niche above the door, which I had seen in old images. 'Oh aye, it fell out and broke,' she said. 'The men came up frae doon south an took it away about twenty year ago.'

I got on the phone to Rab Snowden, the head of the Stenhouse Conservation Centre, and he paused for only a moment and said, 'Oh aye, I remember that. I think it might be in the store ben the hoose.' Later he called me back saying, 'Well, aye, well... it's still here, and it's still in the box we brought it in, unopened. Do you want us to fix it?'

I said no and it came back in two pieces.

The broken piper

Unexpectedly, the panel is made of plaster, not stone, and it does not fit neatly into the niche over the door. It is probably Victorian, so rather than putting it back up there I had a glazed oak display case made for it by Ian Masson, the joiner from Garlogie, who later helped repair the damaged ceilings, and it is now in the Long Gallery. Towards the end of the big project we had it copied in stone and this copy is now in the niche, with a small time capsule behind it for the next time it falls out.

Once most of the conservation policies were in place and the project was well underway, I introduced new challenges to the project team. I needed their advice and support for any decision I had to make. Usually this was simple and we could achieve a consensus fairly readily. Even that day in the grit had been derived from analysis and understanding.

It had become clear from the first discussion that most people considered that the place should be similar to its appearance when it was acquired by the Trust in 1964, but that changes due to accident or negligence should be reversed if possible. There was good enough evidence of the appearance of the castle in the 1820s, including a lovely sketch of the place by James Skene of Rubislaw (1775–1864), an amateur artist, lawyer and a friend of Sir Walter Scott—to make that the touchstone for our decisions, but there was not to be an attempt to recreate the castle at that point. Rather, its appearance then was to guide us today.

This stance allowed me to replace the stone cannons, knocked off in years gone by, but the pragmatic decision not to replace the water spouts was also agreed. The spouts were no longer needed and their replacement would be conjectural, given the great variety of shapes and detailing on those remaining. Also, the cost would have been outwith the budget.

The windows, unblocked in the 1970s, were more contentious. There were conflicting opinions and, it could be said, no right answer. The key was to have a defensible position for whatever course was taken.

The problem was that the removal of an older harl in 1973 had revealed many blocked windows and there was an opportunity to reopen them. Craigievar is far from Edinburgh and the managers were not able to be there quickly, so with the builder keen to get on a decision was hurriedly taken to open them and it was thought by some as we approached our project that this decision had not been fully thought through.

Our research suggested that many of these windows had been originally blocked for carefully considered reasons, towards the end of the eighteenth century. Therefore, it was argued, the unblocking of windows in 1973 had less significance then their blocking. It was possible, therefore, that the re-blocking of the windows would be good conservation practice, but this was not a universally supported position and a great argument arose.

The final decision would be mine and I determined that I needed to have as wide a range of opinions as possible and so a gathering of the knowledgeable and interested was arranged. There were representatives from Historic Scotland, the Royal Commission on the Ancient and Historical Monuments of Scotland, Trust specialists and managers, fundraisers, planners and historians who came to consider the issues and give their opinions.

We all met in one of the cottages where the wonderful property custodian, Daphne, had laid on coffee and cakes. As I stood to begin the session there was a sea of smiling faces. The issues were explained by the team and, in particular, our archaeologist Shannon and her consultant Tom. It was a wonderful day and we toured the scaffolding. Up at the top there was a platform that extended right over the roof where I had thought we might organise a dance one day, but it was raining the day we took the big group up, so that terpsichorean jollity was off the agenda.

After this visit and considering all of the views expressed, my decision was that a representative sample of the many windows unblocked in 1973 should be re-blocked and used as interpretive aids to explain conservation issues to visitors.

The two windows chosen were the most prominent; both are on the turret over the front door. This is the only turret originally designed to have three windows on each floor, and the central one on each level had been blocked

The advisers gather to consider the best colour

at some point in the castle's history, unblocked in 1973, and then re-blocked in 2009, returning the turret to its appearance in the 1820s. The day that the builders closed those windows, I pressed a new 5p coin dated 2009 into the mortar of one, carrying on a tradition of marking dates onto new pieces of work for later generations to discover.

Was re-blocking those windows the right thing to do? I think there was not a wholly correct answer and I could have argued equally forcefully to leave them unblocked. They were part of the initial creation of the castle by the Forbes family and helped to demonstrate the importance of the turret at the top of the complex vertical array of door, armorial and viewing platform in that corner of the castle, all contained within the original courtyard.

To mitigate the change and help interpretation, the internal wall behind these blocked windows was recessed to indicate where the window would have been. In some ways I regret the decision, but it did fit with the overall conservation approach we had during the works and, on balance, I still think it was correct, though others still disagree.

That day with the grit and the mess and the worry that some on the team might not cope with the experience was just a normal day-to-day event, one that soon passed, and the relief was in knowing that this would be so. The windows decision had the capacity to destroy the team, and in such situations a robust process is essential.

It was also a decision that tested the new project guidelines that I had written for the Trust in 2008. I had created a process to resolve difficult decisions, one that would allow the heat to be taken out as colleagues argued ethical and valid opposing views. The process was followed, the issues were resolved and the project moved on. Everyone remained friends and colleagues. The team had been bound together with grit and determination.

17

PINK CASTLE

'Jings, that's gey pink,' was one of the comments from a mason on the new colour of Craigievar. He had just put on the last of six coats of lime wash to the castle walls. With the scaffolding still in place and the building covered in a protective tarpaulin, it was hard to see what the overall effect would be. It was late summer 2009 and the twenty-five-year project to remove the old cement harl and replace it with lime was nearly complete.

A few months earlier we had decided that the colour would be in imitation of the last lime harl from the early nineteenth century, at least as far as we could determine. There are a number of rather lovely images of the place from the time that helped guide us, some in colour and others not. Some correspondence had also turned up suggesting that the colour was similar to the granite and some of the decoration, like the poor wee piper that fell off a dormer window in the 1950s and lost his face.

2009 was a time for reflection. I knew that the whole job might not have happened when, two years earlier just as we were about to begin, the Trust decided that the North East region should be no more. My role as conservation manager would end and I was to lose my employment after twenty-five years.

As the months rolled by it became clear that I would not leave. Rather, I would move back to something similar to my old job as regional surveyor but in a bigger patch and with a small team to manage. So in October 2009 I took up this new role and with it the management of the Craigievar project. I was once more the hands-on project manager. Gavin McCall, who had been the project manager with me as his sponsor, had decided to set up his own business. Fortunately, I was able to appoint him as a consultant on the project.

I visited the site regularly and as I stood high up on the castle walls with the foreman, Stephen Harper, I had a sense that things were going well. This largely arose from working with Stephen. He was young for the responsibilities he had, probably in his late twenties, always smiling.

The team of masons he led were of a similar age, with both men and women on the squad. The contractor business was owned by another dynamic young man with a fierce

Craigievar Castle in 2010

Gavin McCall, Andy Allan and Steven Laing on the Craigievar Scaffolding, 2009

drive to succeed, Steven Laing, whom I had employed on one of his first jobs after he set up his specialist masonry business in the mid-1990s. Steven turned up that first day in the 1990s in his new van, dressed in immaculate bib overall with his health and safety statement in his hand. Builders at that time usually arrived in a beat-up truck, wearing old woollen pullovers with holes at the elbow, a knitted hat on their heads, stubble on their chins and bleary eyes.

Steven gathered his team from near and far to work on Craigievar. There was a wonderful Polish female mason and conservator, and at one point a squad from Malta helped.

We wanted the cement to be removed without mechanical tools and Stephen Harper was asked to use hammers and chisels to get the stuff off. This is not an unusual request. In inexperienced hands mechanical tools can do a lot of damage to historic stonework and can set up vibrations that judder through the walls, and we were all concerned that this might loosen the fragile ceiling plaster.

One day Stephen approached Gavin and me, saying, 'The harl on the north side is gey thick and hard as iron. It'll take an afa time tae take off.' So we agreed to try a mechanical tool.

We measured the vibrations, focusing on the Queen's Room, where I had completed major repairs to the plaster fifteen years or so earlier, and the effect was minimal. In fact, the pounding of a hammer and chisel produced just as much vibration. So we allowed a drill and made good progress. Peter MacLeod, one of Stephen's top men, just newly qualified, soon shone and would later become site foreman at our next big project, at Drum Castle, but that is another tale.

As the team removed the cement, we saw that the masons in 1973 had cut corners, and that made our lives a little easier. Usually those applying

Stephen Harper and Jamie Davidson (aged 11) 2009

a new cement harl to an old building will remove the small stones between the larger boulders; these were used originally to create a flattish surface. The new cement would then be pushed into the space and as it hardened it would grip the big stones, but this makes it very difficult to remove, with cement squeezed into every neuk. However, at Craigievar they had not done this and under the cement most of the original stones and mortar were pretty much intact. Discovering this was a great relief to Stephen, Peter, Gavin and me, not just because it was easier to remove but mainly because a lot of the historic fabric was still in place.

The masonry that was uncovered was rather beautiful. The large boulders were well chosen to create the desired sculptural effect and the mortar and small pinning stones packed around them were mostly untouched, probably from the hand of the mason in the sixteenth century.

When the cement was off a full inspection of the walls was possible and with so little damage to the historic fabric Tom Addyman, our architectural historian, along with the Trust archaeologist, Shannon Fraser, asked the key question. What happened in the early seventeenth century after the place was acquired from the Mortimers by 'Danzig Willie' Forbes?

Craigievar had been owned by the Mortimer family before Danzig Willie made his fortune, but it was not clear what the castle was like at that time. Both Shannon and Tom determined that Forbes had remodelled the top of the building from the fourth storey upwards. The glorious array of turrets, balustrades, roofs, platforms, ornate cannons and spouts were theirs. It was as if they had sliced the top off the old tower like a boiled egg and replaced it with the renaissance display.

Tom's team produced wonderful drawings to help with his analysis and on these we were able to see the many cracks that snake over and through the stonework. We called upon our engineer John Addison, who had been involved with many of our projects and whose pragmatic conservative approach was just what we needed.

The cracks were entirely related to changes in window sizes, particularly in the nineteenth century. They could be seen darting from one window opening to another on the building itself and on Tom's drawings. I was not overly concerned. Buildings of this age always have cracks and, as they appeared to have been stable for decades, I thought there was little chance that Craigievar would become a pile of rubble any time soon. John brought me back to reality when he confirmed that the big concern was whether the stones either side of the cracks were loose. If they were, they would have to be removed one by one and built securely back in. As we stood on the scaffolding pondering this, we realised that it could be a long and expensive operation.

I was once again grateful to have such knowledgeable people around me and John's wit helped us. To determine whether a stone would be removed and rebuilt, a sophisticated tool was needed: a lump hammer. A mason would hit a suspect stone and if the sound was 'dink' it was safe and could be untouched, but if there was a 'dunk' it had to be removed and rebuilt.

Throughout that long summer of dust and dirt, the castle was cared for by Daphne the custodian.

Daphs, as I called her, or 'Hello, Dapho,' when I arrived, was just what you need at a property when a big nasty intrusive project happens. Daphne and her cats were always delighted to see the activity, and her delight was expressed from time to time in the superb lunches she would provide in her kitchen for the project team. Her cats were agile climbers and despite our efforts could often be seen high on the scaffolding, or a fluffy grey flash would tear through the castle door if left open.

One day as I travelled to the castle I saw, about ten miles away, a couple of walkers. Students, I thought, and paid no heed to them. When my work at the castle was over I set off down the drive and saw the two young walkers trudging towards me. They looked exhausted and flagged me down. It turned out they were German students who had taken the bus to Alford and asked for directions to the castle without asking how far it was. After getting some guidance they had set off, not realising they had a three-hour walk ahead of them.

'How far to the castle?' they gasped.

'Just over there,' I said, 'but it's closed for repair.'

They looked even more weary and so sad that I got them into the car and drove back to give them a short private tour of the Great Hall. Daphne and her team had the furniture packed away under purpose-made covers, and on entering the Great

John Addison and his lump hammer, 2009

Hall the students were taken aback, imagining they had stepped into a contemporary art installation. The chairs and tables were hidden by their own white paper shrouds and the artefacts were wrapped and carefully boxed around the room. In the kitchen the iron kettles were turned to white paper versions of themselves. 'You should enter this for the Turner Prize,' they said.

Edith packing the collection at Craigievar Great Hall, 2007

I would often appear at the castle with specialists desperate to see the castle undressed. Professor Charles McKean of Dundee University was the last and the most disappointed in this parade. Charles's capacities for language, history, Scottish architecture and the renaissance buildings of Europe seemed boundless. His aspiration was in part to get his European and English colleagues to take the architectural culture of the Scottish renaissance seriously. I had learned of his status a few years earlier, to my embarrassment.

One day, he arrived at Castle Fraser with a tour group of European visitors. They were viewing Scotland's renaissance heritage and as I was standing beside a tall and elegant older man, I asked if he knew much about the subject, assuming they were a group of visitors with a basic interest. 'Yes,' he said in an engagingly patrician voice. 'I am more involved these days since my retirement. I used to be the director of the Courtauld Institute but now I run the Palladio Centre in Vicenza.' I decided to stop talking and listen.

That was not an unusual situation for me; I regularly embarrass myself. Once in 1992 I found myself, at some reception or other, beside a very well-spoken lady who struck up a conversation. It was election time and she asked for my thoughts on what might happen. I tried to maintain a studiously neutral tone but suggested that the Conservative Party were having troubles here in the North East and I could not see them returning. 'Oh,' she sighed 'that's a shame. My brother was the last Tory MP here.'

Quickly changing the subject, I spoke of my recent holiday to Skye. 'How delightful,' she purred. 'What did you see?'

'The ugliest castle.'

'Really?'

'Yes, Dunvegan,' I replied, remembering its harsh Victorian remodelling.

'Oh dear, my brother-in-law is the laird.'

I turned pink first, then quiet.

Charles and I arranged to visit Craigievar at the end of the project while the scaffolding was still in place. That day the snow fell in thick wet flakes and did not want to stop. Soon the castle drive was impassable and we stood at the bottom of the hill, looking at a steep road blanketed in snow under a leaden sky. There was no wind and the silence was all-enveloping.

So off we slithered to the tearoom in Alford where we met with our kindly benefactor, the most knowledgeable individual on the history of Craigievar. Here, over coffee and cake, they debated the place and the many fascinating facts they knew about it. Having learned from my Castle Fraser experience, I simply looked on and listened.

It was our benefactor who had earlier encouraged me to replace the missing stone cannons on the castle walls. Many had been lost and the spectacular array that should bristle around the corbelling was gone. They had been highly decorative and would have been a dramatic part of the silhouette. Most of them had been lost through accident but I was not sure how that might have happened until the winter of 2009-10, when the snow that impeded Charles McKean and me lay thick around the walls of the tower and on the roof. One day, following a brief thaw, a thick sheet on the north side slid off taking one of the remaining original cannons with it. It landed in the deep drift below, undamaged, and we were able to pin it back in place.

There had been one carving that we always knew would be recreated. It was the little piper who should have stood on top of a dormer window over the front door. He fell off in the 1950s and his shattered remains were in the castle cellar, but the poor wee chap could not go back. His face was missing and the repairs done at the time did not seem robust enough for the cold wind that whistles about the place. I thought that we needed to engage an artist or sculptor to recreate him, and after a bit of a search Graciela Ainsworth in Edinburgh was chosen. Graciela is well known to me as a conservator but I knew she often created delightful sculpture too.

So, one day I heaved the old piper into the car and set off for her studio near Leith. A roller shutter door was lifted and Bartok filled the air from an old battered radio. The space was crowded with gigantic masonry heads and torsos, plaster casts and polystyrene packaging. Graciela and I carefully carried the faceless piper to the bench and I felt like a paramedic delivering a beaten-up victim to the surgeon.

The new piper carved by Graciela Ainsworth
(Graciela Ainsworth Conservation)

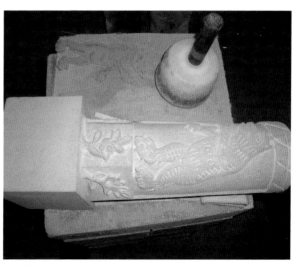

Carving a new cannon for Craigievar Castle, 2009 (McCall Surveying)

The bear from the mazer carved onto a cannon (McCall Surveying)

Soon the new piper would emerge from a block of stone, complete with new face. Our kindly donor was a man with a most interesting hirsute phizog, so photographs were taken of him from several angles and Graciela created a new piper, complete with left-hander pipes and toorie hat, and in midsummer 2009 he was placed on the dormer as the cannons were being fixed in place.

'Now then, Ian,' said our benefactor. 'These new cannons should really be rather intricate and beautiful, don't you agree? Look, there are such wonderful images on the mazer. You will find the original in the Museum of Scotland. That one is a copy.' He pointed at the chalice on the sideboard in the Great Hall. 'I love the bear marching out of the woods with his walking stick.' Mazers were at one time a popular form of drinking bowl, originally made completely out of wood. The Craigievar original is silver and maplewood, made in 1591 and engraved with foliage and animals. The bowl is set on a decorated stem and foot.

As usual, not everyone agreed to have new images on the cannons and the consensus eventually was to replace those that were missing with blank stones, matching the originals in size and shape, but unadorned.

In spring 2009 I had to leave the country to support the National Trust in Western Australia for a couple of months, thinking that on my return the last decision would be to finally agree the new colour for the castle. Before I left we instructed the masons, and a small team of young tradesmen began to make the cannons. While I was away the decision to use blanks was overturned, and when I came back I found a team of young men busily carving them, but I was slightly embarrassed to find that they had carved my initials discreetly onto one, along with the initials of Gavin McCall and John Borland, the Royal Commission artist who had done the drawings from which the carvings were made.

Patchy harl at Craigievar

The young masons had very little experience in carving but they rose to the challenge. 'These are truly magnificent,' said our benefactor. 'Don't you think we should really get on and replace the missing armorial over the door? Nothing too fanciful. I didn't really care for the design Schomberg did in the 1970s; it was far too fussy.'

'Well then,' I suggested, 'let's just copy the one that fell out, even if it wasn't the original.'

Our benefactor and John Borland agreed, especially as we had seen that one of the young masons, Adam Gordon, had an exceptional talent when he carved an intricate interaction of two unicorns on one of the cannons. I hope that Adam keeps this skill throughout his career.

A decision had to be taken on the correct shade of pink that would be applied to the castle walls. This was, I realised, what the whole job would be judged upon. All the planning, arguing, negotiating and researching would be ignored; it was the colour that everyone would notice.

Advisors gathered and we pondered until a shade was selected. It was fairly dark, in an attempt to get close to the shade of the red granite corbelling. Coat after coat was brushed on that summer as ruddy-faced masons worked tirelessly for weeks, but soon a problem arose and I was called out. Within a short space of time the walls had become streaky and we could see the brush marks. To make matters worse, the colour varied wildly, ranging from a near-white to a deep strawberry pink, a bit like a rich strawberry fool—a term I thought might be applied to me.

It looked as if the pigment was migrating to where the brush stroke was heaviest; the light shades were on the upstroke and the dark on the down stroke. What to do? I asked for less pigment in the wash and the unevenness was reduced, though some variation remained, but I did not mind this. I reasoned that we were not seeking a uniform paint finish; it was more 'hand knitted', as I termed it, but we would have to wait for the scaffolding to come down to see whether it had worked. Tense weeks lay ahead. In September the scaffolding began to come down. Section by section the new colour was revealed and it was lovely. The harl glowed in the sun and the sharp corners had been returned where once they were lost.

Craigievar Castle scaffolding

Scaffolding being removed

18

THE PRINCE AND THE PIPER

I was standing on the lawn outside Craigievar with Daphne, the cat-loving custodian of the castle, and the rest of the team, awaiting the arrival of Prince Charles, or, as he is known in Scotland, the Duke of Rothesay. It was party time, the big project was complete and the castle was to be formally reopened to the public. Daphne's cats were locked away to avoid any feline intervention and a small marquee was in place on the only bit of flat ground near the castle. Tiny sandwiches were being handed out and the piper, wearing a full military uniform, complete with Busby, was playing vigorously. The newish CEO gave a short speech while the even newer directors looked on and the project team and contractors mingled with Trust supporters in their summer finery.

We had, for a bit of fun, arranged for the Saltire on the castle to be lowered and the Duke's standard to be raised with a flourish as he arrived.

It was June, the day was delightfully sunny and the piper played on until the sound of a helicopter was heard. It landed on the other side of the hill, where a car awaited and the royal party drove up to the castle. Our lead consultant Gavin McCall had been placed on the top floor of the castle to meet them and it was his role to change the flag.

The party gathered at the front door to greet the Duke and I glanced up at the flagpole as the car appeared in the distance. The Saltire came down. 'Good,' I thought, but a minute or so later I glanced up again to see the pole juddering and shaking with no royal standard being raised. Clearly Gavin was having a problem. The knot on the rope had stuck but with a superhuman effort he fixed it just in time. It whizzed up to whack against the upper pulley, just as the car stopped at the front door and out stepped our guest.

The winter before this happy event had been fierce. Snow had fallen in huge quantities and the tower sat under a white blanket for weeks while the freezing water was slowly seeping into our new harl. This was not good news. Lime can be fragile and takes a long time to harden, so I visited regularly with trepidation and waited to see it all slip onto the ground, like a pair of pink knickers. My fears were groundless and it survived, with only a little fraying around the edges, which we soon patched, ready for the big day.

Everyone had been delighted the previous autumn as the scaffolding was slowly removed to reveal the new pink palace. Each day a little more could be seen and to my delight it

The bagpipe-loving bear of Craigievar

The bagpipe-loving bear of Craigievar and the piper

looked spectacular. The thinness of the harl once more emphasised the light and shade of the sculpture, the new stone cannons created a cannonade that cast crisp shadows in the early morning light, and the weathercock had been re-gilded and sparkled in the sun.

As I looked up at the standard, my eye was drawn to one of the new carved stones on the tower, where I had incorporated a small joke, as a present to the building from the contractor—a new, functioning carved waterspout. There had been one missing over the front that should have taken water from the roof and projected it onto the gravel, away from the vulnerable walls, and we decided to replace it. Our artist suggested that it might be in the shape of a bear, with the water emerging from its muzzle, because the Forbes crest incorporates muzzled bear heads, and we thought this an excellent idea.

The spout would be situated below a dormer window on which sat our newly recreated piper. As it was being carved I stood beside the mason and realised that he was placing the bear's paws beside its ears. Looking from below it would seem that it was covering its ears from the sound of the piper above. 'This cannot be,' I stormed and the paws were then made to cup the ears, the better to hear.

Everyone involved wanted to ensure that the project was properly recognised and a pipe tune was commissioned by the local regional director. Bill Hepburn, the retired Pipe Major of the Turriff Pipe Band was approached. He was delighted and a new 6/8 march was composed, but we wondered what it might be called. Usually there is either a whimsical title for such pieces or at times a pompous one. Names such as 'Pink Castle'

The Duke of Rothesay at the reopening of Craigievar in 2010 (Deeside Photographics)

and 'Dashing the Harl' were suggested, but instead we decided to be pompous and asked the Palace. The tune was eventually named 'The Duke and Duchess of Rothesay's Welcome to Craigievar Castle' and it was played with great verve by the composer's son as the event took place. A framed copy is now on display in the Long Gallery.

The project team wondered how the duke should reopen the place on the day and whether a ribbon should be cut. Daphne, our custodian and ardent royalist, suggested that we wrap the building in a big Forbes tartan ribbon with a huge bow at the front door.

As the royal party made their way along the line of dignitaries, Prince Charles saw the big bow, seemed puzzled by the size of it, and a momentary look of consternation swept across his face. Mustering years of experience and the martial genealogy of his antecedents, he strode forward to meet the challenge. He grasped the monster with two hands and pulled it asunder, the coils of tartan snaking lazily over the gravel in the slight summer breeze.

Pipe tune composed by
P/M William (Bill) G. Hepburn

149

19

THE OLD TOWER

Jim Beddie, the Drum Castle groundsman, always had a drip at the end of his nose when he dug up drains and water pipes around the estate. He had returned to Scotland and the castle in the mid-1970s after a lifetime as a plumber in Canada to marry his childhood sweetheart, working at Drum before retiring to a house surrounded by tall pines that perhaps reminded him of plumbing in the Rockies.

It did not take long after arriving in the Garioch and meeting Jim and other folk before I began to appreciate the changes I had made to my life. Only months earlier I was in Glasgow repairing tenements. Now I was in what felt like a foreign country, where the language of the locals was impenetrable and the oil industry had turned the place into a cosmopolitan jamboree, where you might on the same day see a Texan in his Stetson or a Maori walking through a tiny market town, or indeed a Canadian plumber digging graves beside an ancient castle.

These changes accelerated the loss of Doric, the language of Aberdeenshire. The dialect could still be heard within the Trust, where the gardeners, groundsmen and castle staff were mostly local, Jim being the exception. They were often farm labourers no longer able to find employment on the land.

There was parochialism in the shire, which manifested in a myopic view of international events, mythologised by the apocryphal headlines in the local newspaper which are said to have read when the Titanic sank, 'NE man lost at sea', or on the outbreak of the Great War, 'Giant Neep found in Turriff'. Such headlines were parodied by the *Buchan Observer* in 2016 with 'Aberdeenshire business owner wins presidential election', in reference to Donald Trump, who owns a golf resort in the vicinity. These slightly patronising stories mask a greater truth.

The sense of place was very strong, and while I felt this in Glasgow, it was different here. The urban Scots loyalty is often to the tribe, the small community within the larger whole, rather than the land. In Glasgow this often manifested itself in politics, with the Red Clydeside phenomenon being a good example, or in a commitment to one or other of the two big football clubs, each with an undertone of religious bigotry or, less pejoratively, affiliation. This did not exist in North East

Drum Castle and Tower (Jim Henderson)

Scotland and it is little wonder that the locals looked with bewilderment at the big cities in the south.

Aberdeenshire has always been a place apart; its location and poor transport links to the central belt allowed it a unique identity. The historic trading links to the Hanseatic League or the universities of the Low Countries had long passed but the legacy could still be found in the language of the people and the historic buildings that survived.

I loved to listen to the local dialect and, when I had overcome my own bewilderment, it was a rich source of enjoyment. I would spend time with the gardeners and groundsmen, listening to their intonation and vocabulary. I could find linkages across the north in words like sark, meaning shirt, shared with the Finno-Ugric languages, or haystacks being 'rigs' in the Doric and 'rooks' in the Baltic.

At Drum the tenant farmer, Charlie, was deeply embedded in the community and here I found a route to a greater understanding of the work ethic that is, in some way, different from elsewhere in Scotland and the wry demeanour that is often mischaracterised as 'dour' or 'thrawn'.

The locals are an industrious lot, historically committed to one of the two great industries of fishing and farming. My travels have not taken me into the fishing communities, which still exist in a reduced state along the Moray coast, but they did take me into the farming communities. The age of the horse was still within living memory on the farms in 1983, and the hard lives of the farm labourers were etched in the memories of the men and women I spoke to.

There was often a deep-seated antipathy towards the fairmer and the old feein system of employment, which was a type of indentured servitude. It produced a rich subculture in the bothy ballads, with later tunes such as the comic 'Nicky Tams' being linked to the music hall. Other ballads were directly evolved from farming life and would be performed by a few quietly spoken men who had within their repertoire even older songs from long ago, such as 'The Laird o Drum'.[6]

> The Laird o Drum has a-huntin gane
> All in the mornin early
> And he has spied a weel-faur'd maid
> A-shearin her faither's barley.

I didn't hear this song sung before 2014, when it was delivered at the ceremony to reopen the Old Tower of Drum following its major repairs.

The historic buildings are embedded within their environment at Drum and ancient woodland grows nearby. The Old Wood, as it is known, is one of the last areas of deciduous woodland in the area and is now cared for by the Trust. In my early days I had little to do with it other than as a place to walk and talk to the locals. One was the forester, Philip Littlejohn. Philip had been with the Trust since the 1950s. He lived next to the restaurant at Crathes Castle and patrolled the woods shooting roe deer that were

interfering with the natural regeneration of the trees. I thought I might try shooting with him one day, but he collapsed taking a party through the Old Wood and passed away. Another link was gone.

During those first few months, on a sunny Sunday in 1983, visitors abseiled down the east wall of the Old Tower of Drum on the 660th anniversary of King Robert I awarding the castle to William de Irwin. Small pieces of old harl scattered on the lawn where hundreds gathered to watch medieval jugglers and falconry.

Jim the groundsman had gone away for the weekend but earlier in the week he told me, in his curious Canadian-Aberdonian voice, 'You don't wanna be here or you'll get a job,' muttering about the tidy-up he would face on the Monday.

Despite his warnings I went along and my first Trust summer event started when I was handed a leather pouch and placed on the lawn to sell tickets to the visitors whose cars were queued all the way back to the main road, snaking down the mile-long drive. The car park soon filled and spilled onto the adjacent field. Charlie the farmer moved his beasts into their shed and hundreds of people swept down the hill to the castle. The toilets couldn't cope with the demand and the water supply dried as the big tank on the hill emptied. Everyone seemed happy, though Krista the property manager, who operated on a tightly coiled spring, looked frantic. The calmer heads of the regional factor and director held the place together and I bustled about to little effect.

As the afternoon progressed and the ice cream had nearly sold out, the display of falconry began. A small hawk took to the sky as little children in the crowd struggled to watch it in the bright sunlight. The falconer chirped his call to attract it back to his lure but it would not return. Suddenly it flashed through the sky and smacked into a pigeon. Blood and feathers fell onto the crowd and there were gasps from the kids as the hawk took its dinner to the lawn. Dick Hillson, the regional director, had organised the day and took control, offering the remaining ice cream to any traumatised kid.

Dick's events had a dedicated following and caused Aberdeenshire to be the most densely populated membership area in the Trust, which it remains to this day. His style was unique. Each working day around mid-morning he would arrive at his office within Pitmedden House from his apartment next door. Then would then sit for about an hour dictating letters and memos, following which he would return to his apartment. Sometimes, later in the day, he would make visits to the properties.

Drum Castle before the Trust acquisition

The last resting place of Torty the Tortoise (IMD)

One day in autumn that year Jim asked if I liked plums. 'Yes,' I said and large boxes began to appear in my car. The crop in the disused walled garden, where they grew untamed among the dilapidated glasshouses, was bigger than usual and Jim was trying to offload as many as possible. As a single twenty-three-year-old living alone, I was not sure what to do with them but they kept me regular for weeks.

Jim's enthusiasm for digging up pipes had another outlet when he had to dig graves, not in the family plot behind the old chapel, but when called upon to bury the family pets. The Irvines created a pet cemetery beside the human one and tiny gravestones would appear bearing the names of dogs that had lived in the castle. The family moved away in 1976 with their pets, who returned only when their time came to be taken to this plot.

One day in 1988 I was unsurprised to find Jim trudging along, baseball cap clamped down on his head and with his shovel over his shoulder. He was off to the pet cemetery. 'Another pooch has passed,' I mused. Not this time. It was Torty who had turned up his toes. Torty the tortoise had arrived over 140 years earlier and when the family left he went too, surviving another few years. His stone bears his name and his age and I take visitors to see it when I am in the chapel.

The chapel is remote from the castle in a stretch of woodland where small leaded, stained-glass windows cast colourful light into the gloomy interior. During a visit to the building around 1990, I noticed that the larger window had a curious deformation. It was bellied out, as if a divine wind from within the structure had pushed on it. Fortunately, I had experience with stained glass, having had the huge windows in the Haddo Chapel re-leaded, but I could not understand how this curious damage might have happened. The usual deformation occurs as they slump under their own weight and the lower panes buckle.

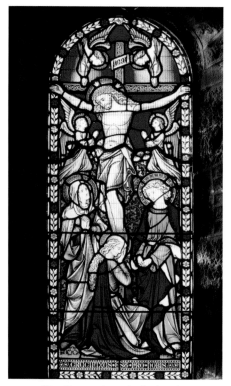

The Drum chapel window by Hardman & Co (IMD)

It was a surprise for the castle manager, Krista, who ran the castle with determined rigour. Every day the stone floors in the castle were scrubbed and no speck of dust would dare to lie for long on the furniture. Soon I realised that the curious problem with the chapel window arose from this enthusiasm for cleanliness. Unbeknown to Krista, when the cleaner mopped the floor of the chapel she would dicht the window with the mop at the same time. Martin Farrelly, the leaded glass specialist, who helped fix the Haddo windows, came along to help and we soon got it straight again.

There has been no more mopping of the windows since.

Krista usually dressed in variations of black and white. She was tall and thin, smoked heavily and had a fierce reputation for efficiency and probity. With her bobbed straight black hair I could have imagined her dancing the tango with severity, though with the occasional sparking smile. She was German and married to a large, gregarious Scot. Theirs was a partnership of seeming opposites that created a firm and lasting bond—a true love match.

She had arrived in 1983 when the roof was being re-slated and the mess did not faze her, nor was she happy about the dirt and disruption when the Jacobean Mansion was to be reharled.

The Trust's area surveyor, Bill Hanlin, had brought me to the team set to take on this task, working with the architect Bill Jack from St Andrews, who had the unique distinction of being an architect in private practice and a government historic building inspector. He was getting on in years when he was at Drum and could not climb ladders, so during site visits he inspected the works from a shooting stick seat with a small telescope, much to Krista's amazement. She had worked with architects before, perhaps back in Germany, and had never seen the like.

In the early 1980s the preferred material for harling a castle was cement, usually with a chemical colour added. The two Bills decided that they should ask the remaining members of the Irvine family what the colour of the castle had been in their youth, so they consulted James Irvine, a lovely old country gent, who would twinkle slightly when Krista appeared and who was quietly spoken and considerate to a Glasgow oik like me.

James was sure that it was a dark red. 'Burgundy,' he said, so the weathervane turret and the chimneys were used as a test. The two Bills arrived to assess the colour, Bill the architect bringing his shooting stick to sit on and the other Bill doing the driving.

We all gathered on the lawn and cringed when the harling was ready for inspection. The raspberry red was overpowering and James, his cousin Toby the Laird of Straloch, Nick Bogdan from Barra Castle at Oldmeldrum and the two Bills all agreed that a lighter tone was essential. I would see that same dark colour many years later, during a lecture tour in Malacca, where the British colonial buildings were painted dark red. I wondered if James had perhaps been there during the war, but that was pushing my imagination a little too far.

After the mansion was harled, in 1986, the Old Tower would be re-pointed rather than reharled. This structure stood in a sad semi-derelict state when the Trust took over.

Remnants of an old harl could be seen on the walls but everyone agreed that the exposed stonework should remain and an 'ancient monument' style recessed point was specified.

By this time Bill Jack had retired and a younger colleague had taken over. The other Bill asked me to take control of the local issues and I met with the Historic Scotland architect, John Knight and the inspector, Richard Emerson.

Standing at the foot of the tower they engaged in a little banter. 'We really want to keep those patches of harl on the corners and I want to see some test panels and then you should...'

The other interjected, 'Oh, my. This is the National Trust, after all. We should just let them get on with it.'

I wasn't sure how deep the irony was in those comments.

Everyone wanted to use lime mortar instead of cement by this time, but I am pretty sure that the builders had little faith in it and added cement to make it harden.

Throughout all of this the Irvine family were pleased to have been involved and when the curators decided to create a nursery in the castle they donated some of their own childhood treasures. Unfortunately, the original nursery was not available and so a room further up the stair was used. James came to see it and I think he was delighted. Sadly, he passed away shortly afterwards.

Our curators seemed to be enthused by the nursery at Drum, which was created at a time when similar displays were appearing at Brodie and Kellie Castles. The

Drum Castle with red chimneys

curatorial enthusiasm for Drum was whetted and they turned their eyes to the Old Tower.

Poor Krista was, by this time, a little punch-drunk from the stream of repairs whirling around her but she stood firm, keeping the staff together and the castle immaculate. Krista, her husband and daughter lived in a flat on the top floor of the castle. It too was immaculate, as I had suspected, and really warm.

Krista Chisholm (Jim Henderson)

She did not care for the cold and my surveying predecessor had installed a new heating system, which she used ruthlessly.

One day I was called to see a trickle of dust that had appeared in the display dining room below her apartment, spoiling the immaculate setting of the sideboard. No matter how often it was dusted more appeared. Krista was not pleased. The ceiling above was panelled in a reddish hardwood rather than plastered and the heat created in Krista's flat had warped the boards and allowed a steady trickle of lime dust to drift down. I had a little mastic filler applied and the dust stopped. It's still there and Krista was pleased, which meant everyone was happy.

Krista rolled her eyes at the thought of rewiring the castle when I suggested it a few years later. After doing similar projects at several other properties, I was not immune to the curatorial method of prioritisation through enthusiasm, trying each time to follow the advice of the Society for the Protection of Ancient Buildings; I was a Scottish committee member and enthralled by its rules.

Our electricians were local and were both tidy and conscientious. They worked for a long-established firm managed by a softly spoken man from Inverurie. Whenever I was getting something wrong he would whisper, 'Ooo, aye, have ye ever thought of...', gently putting me on the right track. He was supported by a tall, rugby-playing sparkie, Colin, who would unfold his giant frame from small spaces under floors and in attics and who remains a great tradesman with the same firm. We played rugby together, though I have to admit that he was in a different class to me and continued in the local first team into his fifties.

By the time the wiring was done I could see that Krista, and indeed the castle, had taken enough and I determined to direct my efforts elsewhere. When I visited again in 1994, I was stopped short while walking down from the car park. The sunlight was bright and high, and on the wall of the old tower was a dark patch.

Damp, the surveyor's nightmare!

20
DAMP PATCH

I stood in the car park at Drum and stared. I may even have been slack jawed. There was a big damp patch in the middle of the wall of the Old Tower, not at the top where a roof leak might be the cause, and high enough to mean it was not rising from the ground. It was in the middle of the wall.

I realised this was at the level of the earth floor in the High Hall and water was finding its way down through the core of the wall until it reached this point, creating a reservoir then seeping to surface where I could now see it.

The tower would have been damp for over 700 years and in its early days the movement of people living there and the lighting of fires to keep them warm would have kept the place dry. It was largely abandoned in the early seventeenth century and it had sat unoccupied since. The ancient interiors, especially in the old High Hall, were left to the elements, the window openings were unglazed and the timber floors and the doors were removed. The High Hall slowly deteriorated and the medieval screens passage collapsed, slowly immersing itself into the earth floor.

This gentle neglect ended in the 1850s when the library was created in the Laigh Hall, below the High Hall, which, in itself, created interesting problems, but I will come to that later.

The historic dampness in the tower was never a big problem over the centuries. The top of the parapet around

The Old Tower damp patch

Damp and decaying books in Drum Library

the walkway had allowed water to seep through the joints to the core of the walls since the castle was built, but it would evaporate through the walls and a lime render or harl would act like a big poultice, allowing it to dissipate.

By re-pointing the tower with a dense mortar in 1986, this equilibrium had been interrupted and the evaporation had stopped. It was clear in 1994 that something must be done, and a big project began its tortoise-like progress through the Trust's systems.

Krista, the manager, would have been ready for the challenge but she moved on long before any real progress could be made. The property then suffered from several years of limited management and without Krista and her single-minded dedication there could be little support from the property-based staff. I wondered what else I could do. The next cyclical resurvey of the castle ensured that the problem was highlighted and therefore became a priority for grant funding.

The biggest push came after I had appointed a collections specialist for the region in 2000. This lady was to be crucial in winning hearts and minds. She was part of a profession that was fairly new to the Trust and she enthusiastically took up the challenge. Among the first of her objectives was recording changes in the artefacts in each property between cleaning operations. This was a massive undertaking, as there are thousands of items to be examined, but at Drum it was a great opportunity to have the books in the library, which is in the Old Tower, taken out, dusted and recorded. The process was repeated the following year, and Krista's successors made an unexpected and worrying discovery.

A row of books were mouldy and some were disintegrating. We knew there had been no changes to the building and the only variable was humidity. It seemed that the damp in the walls was now affecting the moisture in the air of the library. The volunteers got to work and the collections care staff rallied around. The library became a surgery for the books, which were carefully removed onto acid-free tissue paper, inspected and gently cleaned and then placed in a store elsewhere in the castle on archive shelving especially bought for this purpose. My attempts to have the tower repaired now had added momentum. Even without Krista and her drive we could get stuck in.

Then, one day around 2007, a donor approached the Trust. 'I think I would like to support your good works,' he said on the phone from America.

So those kind people in the fundraising team included the Old Tower on the list he was sent and a query soon arrived for me. 'How

Removing the damp books from the Drum Library

much will it cost? We need to say this afternoon.'

This is a question where the answer should not be guessed but I had no choice. So surrounding my answer with caveats, and basing it on the cost of repairing Craigievar, which was underway, I made my best guess even though I knew I would not be able to escape this figure and it would hang around my neck like an albatross. I took a deep breath and named my price.

The damp was by this time the overriding worry at Drum, but other issues would sometimes raise their

Damp damage to books in the Drum Library

head and, as the regional deputy director, I could find myself in uncomfortable places. The Old Wood would come back into my consciousness once more.

Philip Littlejohn the gentle forester had long since passed away before I became more closely involved with the Old Wood. The roe deer that had been his bane were mostly under control and regeneration was happening. It was 2006 and I was briefly the interim regional countryside manager. The previous incumbent found another job and as I was his manager I had to fill in for about six months—something I was supremely unqualified to do.

One opportunity, however, was to become better informed about the wood, where a survey of the habitats and species was being prepared. The authors were surprised when two rare and curious rhododendrons were found. They were not the ubiquitous *Rhododendron ponticum* but were strange and rather lovely. Could it be, they wondered, that the Irvines of Drum had tried to improve the Old Wood with a bit of foreign colour?

'Not really,' said the surviving brother of the last laird. He recalled he had been asked to dispose of them as a lad and got tired carrying them, so they were surreptitiously dumped deep in the undergrowth where they survived the decades till they were formally recorded.

I had a very minor role in the commissioning of another report on the Old Wood as a medieval woodland pasture. The theory was that the Lairds of Drum might have maintained their herd in the woodland and the report thought it likely. 'How interesting,' I thought, as the document slid over my desk on its way to someone who could understand it better than me (not particularly difficult).

A few days later I found myself, along with the regional director, at a dinner in Mar Lodge as the guest of a Dutch conservation body. He did not much care for these events and swapped the place cards, so I found myself at the head of the table between the chairman and chief executive and their partners. It was a lovely evening until one asked if I knew anything about the Old Wood, as they had been there that day and there had been very little information. 'Why yes,' I said and told them the little I had gleaned from the report on the woodland pasture concept, thinking to myself that I had blagged my way out of a tricky corner. The chairman tapped his glass with a spoon to quiet the crowd and announced that I would give an after-dinner

The old wood, Drum Castle

speech on the Old Wood. The regional director had a wicked smile on his face and I knew I had been set up.

I was able to gather myself and spoke, passing quickly over the report, as I realised that by saying it might have been a woodland pasture there was little more I could have added. Continuing to address the gathering, I recalled a time around 2002-03 when I arrived at Drum, late and out of breath, where I had been due to meet a large group of archaeologists. I strode purposefully over the lawn and the relieved Trust archaeologist asked me to explain why there was a large damp patch on the west elevation of the Old Tower.

I said, 'If it wasn't for the lascivious intentions of a dirty old man, who happened to be a medieval king, there would be no damp patch today.' The lady archaeologist looked a little shocked. I went on to explain, mischievously, that the king was Alexander III, who famously died in a riding accident on his way back to his new young wife.

The consequence of that late-night escapade was that his niece, Margaret, Maid of Norway, was to be brought to Scotland and crowned, but she died on the boat leaving no heir. This led to the Wars of Independence, won eventually by Robert the Bruce, who then gave Drum to his clerk, William de Irwin. The Irvines lasted 700 years and then the Trust took over. We repaired the tower with the wrong kind of mortar and a damp patch appeared eight years later. The link was clear to me: no fall from a horse, no acquisition by the Trust, no damp patch!

Recounting that anecdote saved my skin at the Mar Lodge dinner, and everyone seemed happy as the evening progressed.

Thinking back to that discussion with the archaeologists and having explained the big damp patch, I was asked how old the tower was. 'Late thirteenth century,' I asserted, placing it in the period of Alexander III. I was challenged for evidence, but there was none other than family tradition and the guesswork of historians, repeated daily to visitors by the castle guides. That damp patch and the query about the age of the old place were to dominate the next few years.

During the early 1990s I once visited the Old Tower with the Trust president Lord Wemyss, who had served the National Trust for Scotland from 1946 to 1991, first as chairman of the Council and then as president, and his son Lord Neidpath. They enthusiastically explored the tower, striding briskly around as I pointed out the blocked door that would have led into the Laigh Hall that was now the library. They were more excited to find the medieval toilet in the High Hall and the ancient window seats. The father missed out the terrifying precipitous timber stair rising in a single flight of about thirty steps up to the walkway and the crenulated wall head. He asked if there were any hidden rooms and I said there were none that I knew of. I would be proven wrong, many years later.

Lord Wemyss thought that placing the library in the Old Tower was curious. 'Forming a library in a damp draughty tower seems a brave decision,' he said. 'Surely it could not have seemed very damp at the time.'

I suggested that the High Hall above would have been draughty and the long slow decline of the medieval interior must have reached a stasis. Placing the library there would not have been seen as much of a risk.

When the damp patches appeared in the 1990s and water could be seen trickling into the building as if into a subterranean cavern, the question was how to manage this damp and whether there was any evidence from the past that might guide us.

In 2012 we appointed a team with experience in analysing ancient buildings and their initial reports found evidence that the damp may have become a concern soon after the library was inserted in the 1850s. They tried, it seemed, to fix this by harling the walls but after about twenty years the harl fell off, leaving some small remnants still visible today.

By now a big project was underway and there was a lot of interest, so I invited as many people as possible into the dining room of the castle to discuss the work we needed to do. They gathered on a chilly February day and the next property manager, Gareth, who also managed Crathes a few miles away, plied us with coffee and biscuits. The Trust curators and conservators, interpretation planners and archaeologists were there and some non-staff came too, including Historic Scotland architects and historians. The biggest concern for the group was what the tower would look like after the repairs were finished.

The day seemed to go quite well, with strong opinions expressed and many people not wanting the appearance of the place to be changed too much. The allure of a rubbly castle was strong. I was an advocate for harling and others took a different view, but one point was made that would force me to think differently.

The tower was caught in a paradox. It was like an ancient ruin where you don't need to worry about the internal environment, but the library in the middle of the tower created a situation where, while managing the ancient monument, we also had to maintain museum-like conditions in the middle.

Drum Castle in 1884, by Andrew Gibb

I thought that a new harl would assist in drying the tower, massively increasing the area through which the water might evaporate. When it became clear that my decision was likely to be to reharl, there was uproar. The weight of opinion was that people liked the rubble and did not want it covered. The rugged appearance gave the place the gravitas of age, and as I stood my ground it was like being in a hailstorm without a coat. I had to think again.

The view opposed to harling the tower was very important, but I found that there was not enough evidence for me to secure a defensible conservative position for any decision I made. The key to finding an acceptable repair strategy is to weigh the evidence, determine the significance of the issues, undertake a comparative analysis and reach a decision that can be objectively justified. If I could demonstrate that the rugged appearance of the tower was a deliberate aesthetic choice, caused either by the accidental loss of the harl or by not replacing it, I could give significance to the rubble appearance and help to justify its retention.

I could not find any such evidence. I might have argued that harling the tower after the insertion of the library suggested that the aesthetic choice of the family was for a harled building. However, in the 1870s, the family had formed a new entrance hall to the occupied part of the house. Here they created a rubble exterior using a technique known as sneck harling where only the joints of the masonry have a covering, suggesting they liked a rubble appearance on the building. Earlier, in the 1850s, they had removed plaster from the ground floor of the mansion and had done the same in the chapel, leaving the masonry exposed.

I suspect that, in both these earlier cases, this was the result of damp but it probably fitted within the mid-nineteenth century fashion known as 'rubblemania'[7] that exposed stonework that was never meant to be seen.

I struggled on with voices calling for a particular answer and no clear direction identified through research and planning, so I called upon a smaller group of experts from within and outwith the Trust for advice.

We realised that the harling of the tower in the 1870s could have been a pragmatic solution to a new damp problem in the library or it might have been a design choice. It was not possible to say. When the harl began to fall off no attempt had been made to keep it, which may have been an aesthetic judgement, but was probably because of the cost.

All in all, I could not come to a conclusion on what the cultural significance of the rubble appearance of the tower was, and in the end the decision was a practical one. If the Victorian harl had failed so quickly and so spectacularly, could I take the risk of a similar experience now? Could I justify the expense of a full harl in expectation that it would fall off within a few decades? I decided against reharling, and a rather mannered approach was adopted that did not try to recreate an earlier appearance, but would address the damp while offering the best chance of longevity. The most important factor was how best to manage the damp for the benefit of the tower and the library within it.

Soon it was time for the scaffolding to go up.

21

KING ROBERT'S THRONE

The archaeologists had removed stones blocking tiny windows high up on the Old Tower at Drum. These openings were remnants of the earliest days of the castle, and as I made my way over I thought of Lord Carnarvon and Howard Carter at the tomb of King Tut.

Carter peered into the tomb.

'Can you see anything?' Carnarvon asked him.

'Yes,' he replied. 'Wonderful things.'

Jonathon our archaeologist peered into the opening.

'Can you see anything?' I asked.

'Yes,' he replied, and we all leaned forward in anticipation.

Unlike Carnarvon, I was not in a pale Homburg hat, urging the diggers on. Rather, I was in a high-visibility jacket and plastic hard hat.

It was possible to remove these stones in the summer of 2013 only because a big team pulled together. Bill, the appropriately named quantity surveyor, was key to the success of the project and this would be his last job before retirement.

Bill dressed soberly in the uniform of the country professional, with pens aligned along the top pocket of his tweed jacket. One winter day, wearing his anxious expression along with his uniform, he had come over to my office at Castle Fraser, weighed down with the heavy bundles of priced tenders for us to open. Bill whispered, 'Are they too low?'

I tried not to sound too pleased. 'No,' I replied. 'Not at all.'

Letters to accept the lowest offer were prepared.

I was later at a meeting in Edinburgh about something else entirely when my mobile phone buzzed. With an apologetic face, I surreptitiously sneaked a look at the screen under the table. The over-bright light shone out. 'Do not make the appointment,' was the message from the solicitor.

Good grief. Time might be money but it is also unremitting in its forward march, and if we didn't start soon the programme would be at risk. I knew the mortar must have time to set before winter and any delay could be catastrophic. Each day I would speak

Archangel Michael by Hugh Irvine (1783-1829)

Revealing the hidden chambers at Drum Castle

confidently to the bemused contractor till the next phone message confirmed, about a month late, 'There is no problem. Please proceed.'

Stephen, the contract manager, uttered a comforting, 'Aye, aye, nae bother, aye,' when we looked at the revised programme, but he seemed worried.

The project team gathered at the castle to consider the new programme, followed by a trip into the library in the core of the Old Tower. We climbed the grey granite stair to the first floor to the Cross Chamber, stopped to pose for a photograph and then went into the dark, brown library, where the sight that greeted us made us gasp. Everything was sheathed in white; it was like walking into a paper bag.

A team of elderly volunteers had worked in near sub-zero conditions covering the books and paintings to keep any dust away during our project. I had seen plumes of vapour rise from their breath while they worked in shifts with breaks for hot drinks in a warm room.

The previous autumn, Alison, the property manager—Krista's successor after that unfortunate period of limited management—had asked me to give them and the staff a talk about the tower and one volunteer asked if the library chimney would be fixed and the fire used again. They liked the heat and so did I, so I said yes.

The fire had to be abandoned that year when smoke began to seep into the courtyard through the flue walls and as the query was raised I could feel a collective leaning forward in anticipation as my response was awaited. The property manager looked inquisitive and I hoped we would be able simply to find the hole and fill it.

Standing there in that pregnant pause before saying yes, my thoughts flashed back to Krista, the previous manager, who detested the cold. Throughout the 1980s she would have the fire blazing and I had watched the burr walnut mantelpiece warp under the blast.

Normally a visitor might not look at that fireplace, despite its wonky mantle, for above it hangs a most peculiar self-portrait, by Hugh Irvine (1783-1829), depicting him floating in the sky as the Archangel Michael. It is often called Gabriel, but I believe it to be Michael, who is represented as an angelic warrior, carrying a spear. The portrait is not the most arresting feature; Hugh Irvine is naked but for a tiny wisp of ribbon to cover his embarrassment. His calm yet strangely maniacal gaze looks into the middle distance. Perhaps the heat rising from below has warped him too.

The curators had moved a number of the paintings throughout the castle in the early 1980s, but their improving eye did not stop there. The pinkish bookcases offended them and I was persuaded to have them grained to a dark oak.

David L., the curator, called me to his side. He was dressed in his usual yellow crewneck pullover with tie poking over the top, green cord trousers and the most highly polished brogues outside of the Guards. 'These are rather dowdy,' he said, looking sadly at the bookcases, then turning to me as, apparently, the fount of wisdom—flattery was one of his many weapons—he asked, 'Don't you think they could use a bit of a birthday? How about a grain, something dark to knock it back a bit and give the place some authority, hmmm?' The last inquisitive sound was uttered on a rising note infused with a hint of coercion around a note of instruction.

'Let's use that nice man from Inverurie,' he suggested, so we engaged Ally, who had become a favourite after I had him disguise a plywood panel at Crathes.

So pink became brown and everyone seemed very pleased.

David L. moved on from the Trust in the late 1990s, but those library shelves would become the backdrop for a display of even stranger paintings.

In 2013 I was standing inside this room-sized paper bag, the woodwork draped in dustsheets, when Alison, the new manager, grasped my arm. She stared me straight in the eye and declared enthusiastically, 'Wouldn't it be wonderful for an exhibition?'

'No' was not an acceptable answer and resistance was futile. Alison's irresistible force was to be directed later to the creation of a gallery for temporary exhibitions, under the attic bedrooms. I thought this would be wonderful, as it would give access to the Long Gallery where some of the massive seventeenth century panelling with chunky bolection mouldings and gigantic fireplaces remained. So we made it happen.

Alison persuaded Aberdeen Art Gallery to bring their collection while their exhibition space was being renovated, and in 2015 Drum housed a gruesome portrait by Ken Currie, one of the 'New Glasgow Boys', whose unsettling portrayals of the body often depict illness and decay. As I said at the time, I would not want to live in his head.

That exhibition arrived after the big project and drew a crowd, but the scaffolding on the tower attracted its own trickle of tour groups and students. I am not sure what Peter the foreman thought of all these visitors. A son of the manse, his quiet demeanour hid a steel core and I have seldom seen a project with such close attention to safety. I even had to buy a new pair of boots!

If asked for anything, Peter's response was either a brisk 'Aye, sure, aye,' or 'Noooo,' delivered in an assessing slow drawl with a keen eye on you to be sure that it was understood. Peter was great and he found a new skill when we arranged for school groups to visit to see the men at work. With Peter in the lead and me at the back, we would take them up the scaffolding, all the way to the top, to their squealed delight.

Peter and I would walk around the tower every week, finding new things that entranced us, though the outlet from the ancient toilet off the walkway, to my eye at least, resembled a bahookie.

More prosaically, Jonathon the archaeologist found remnants of an ancient harl and tiny remnants were everywhere, once you knew where to look. He was a quiet, bespectacled man in middle years, lean from running up and down scaffolding, and he had an ability to make those with him feel clever. We had agreed that some tiny windows should be unblocked, so Peter took his chisel and carefully removed the stonework filling the small apertures. They peered in and decided that a call to my office should be made.

I stood on the scaffolding and inquired anxiously, 'Can you see anything?'

Jonathon replied, 'Yes, a medieval toilet.'

Taking the torch, I peered in and had to declaim, 'It's King Robert's throne.' The archaeologists looked on with that pitying smile that I have come to recognise.

'Come to the other side. It gets better,' they said and we clambered around to the west where another small window had been unblocked. Peering through, I could see a small room and beyond this a door to another room, all within the thickness of the wall.

We had discovered the buttery. Once more I demonstrated my ignorance. 'Was that were the dairy food was kept?' Shannon the Trust archaeologist, with great forbearance, explained to me that this was where the booze was stored, in butts, or barrels, and that the butler would have held the key. 'Ah,' I said, a little shamefaced.

Everyone called these newly discovered rooms the 'secret chambers', to the annoyance of the archaeologists; they were hardly secret since the windows were always there to see, but everyone likes a mystery. The TV folk even managed to tie their camera to a long stick and poke it through the window of the buttery, hoping to look around the corner into the pantry, where the 'pan', or bread for those Norman nobles, might have been stored.

That word, 'pan', lasted into my childhood in Glasgow, where if you were a bit better off you might buy a pan loaf or if you spoke with a Kelvinside accent you were 'awfy pan loaf', as my Granny might have said.

Gavin, our consultant, Bill the quantity surveyor, and Peter the son of the manse would meet me regularly in the nearby garden centre tearoom to assess progress and plan ahead, usually focusing on money and safety. However, that autumn Peter dropped a bomb. 'I dinna think the lime will make it through the winter without a cover.' This meant the scaffolding had to stay up and the place would be a building site into the next visitor season. The delay at the beginning of the project had done its worst.

'Bang, whizz, crash, wallop,' was the sound of the flak whizzing around my head as budgets had to be redone and brides cancelled

School party with Peter MacLeod

their spring wedding bookings at the castle. It was a time of many meetings and reports, and the strength within the team held everything together.

Peter got to work and soon everything that could be tied down was secure and we were ready for the winter. Huge tanks of water were secured to the bottom of the scaffolding to stop it moving and we awaited the worst that Aberdeenshire might throw at us.

The Old Tower 'bahookie' garderobe

A storm struck on Christmas Eve. I listened to the roar and crash of branches being torn from trees, but our tower stood firm through it all. Later I would tentatively climb up looking for damage to the new mortar but there never was any. The protection was working and in the spring the cover was removed.

Slowly the tower was revealed, and day by day a little more could be seen. The sun always seemed to be shining and the colour looked delightful. A huge collective sigh of relief was heard.

Still we were not finished, and I wondered with despair if this project would ever end. The courtyard was to get a new tar surface in the autumn of 2014, to be sure the place was ready for the Christmas Fair, but before this the archaeologists were to do a bit of digging. This time Jonathon would not be in the trench; it would be Charlie and Hillary of Murray Archaeological Services, the archaeologists from Methlick.

Three wonderful excavations were carried out. Charlie, in a laconic Irish accent, would quietly explain what was to be seen in the mud. Hillary, his wife, would come over, her bright, highly colourful hair drifting in the wind, to add further illumination to my ignorance.

On the very first day and with the very first shovel of earth removed, a medieval cesspit was found, below the throne. Down and down they dug, but sadly no crown or coin was found. It must have been dug out regularly, for understandable reasons.

On the other side of the tower, we wanted to prepare for a path at a spot on the lawn where there might have been a structure, possibly a gatehouse building. Sure enough, there it was under the grass and I hoped that this discovery might answer a conundrum.

In the tower there is a short remnant of an old wooden stair, with just a few treads left. I had first come across it in the cellar in 1983, propped against a wall, and thought little more of it. However, the new millennium arrived and we had a regional archaeologist and collections conservator who knew that it was special. Timber dating was done which told us it was made from a tree cut down in the fifteenth century. Wonderful, we all agreed. It might be the oldest ladder in the Trust's collection.

King Robert's throne, the hidden toilet

Window of King Robert's throne room

When Jonathon the project archaeologist had a look, he recognised that it was made from old roof timbers. There must once have been a fifteenth century building at Drum, but there was none now. Could it have been that gatehouse? I still don't know.

Finally Charlie and Hillary moved to a side door where a ramp might be needed to help the less able get into the castle, so we had a look to see what might lie below. This final investigation was the most anxious for me.

At the beginning of the project I had to decide if the remnants of ancient mortar should be retained on the walls while newer stuff was replaced in lime. I decided that it should, since it was not causing the damp problem and it allowed anybody who looked to see a little of the many changes to the appearance of the old place.

There is a big patch of very old mortar on the south wall, near the side door where the ramp was to be installed. I wondered if this patch could delineate a building that once stood there. Shannon was convinced and I decided to take a chance and keep this patch in the hope that it might be. But what if we were wrong? We would be left with a big ugly patch of old mortar within the neat new pointing around it. We decided to take the chance, but would I be left with a big mortar-filled egg on my face?

It turned out that there was evidence of an older building there, just as Shannon the archaeologist predicted, and I was egg free!

Huge diggers rolled into the courtyard and the old tar was soon gone. Underneath was a mass of drains and cables and it was a nightmare. Every day brought a new

Murray Archaeological Services explore the ground at the base of the Old Tower (MAS)

challenge and I was knee-deep in mud and water too often for comfort. It was awful. The men digging hated it; they were used to working in the wide open spaces, not cramped wee castle courtyards where their every move was watched by teams of archaeologists and pasty-faced, anxious project managers. I could feel myself age each day as they slowly edged their way out onto the drive and stopped.

There was one question everyone was asking. 'Finished yet?' No, we were not finished. There was still that bloody chimney to do. The original aspiration to find and fill the hole that had been letting the smoke out was forlorn. The whole flue now needed to be relined and I could have cried. More trials and tests followed and we decided to coat the walls of the flue with a fireproof substance, rather than push a metal liner up. I had doubts, but in a few days it was done, the fire was lit and happy, smiling faces could be seen in the glow emanating from the hearth.

Later that summer there was a party on the lawn. The laird arrived to a fanfare of drumming arranged by Alison. Songs were sung and the tower was formally reopened. I sneaked away into the castle to sit quietly, listening to the hubbub and pleased the job was done.

22

THE MUCKLE STEEN

In my time there have been three grass cutters at the Trust's properties in Aberdeenshire. Sandy was first, a gentlemanly former farm servant who was tall and thin with a slightly stiff gait as he made his way around the lawns. Then there was Hamish, but only for a wee while, and then Alan. They travelled around the shire with a big mower keeping the grass around the castles under control.

Each would go to Leith Hall when needed and whizz around, except for Sandy whose stately progress was nothing less than graceful, until there was a crunch under the blades as they hit a big stone under ancient trees close to the house. Each would then clamber down, remove their woollen bunnet, scratch their head, look at the chipped blade and vow to miss that bit next time.

Doddie the gardener—Doddie being a local nickname for George—stood beside Sandy in the 1980s, after the first crunch of the blades where the muckle steen stuck out, and decided he had better things to do than attack it with a spade and a pick. His successors did the same, so the stone was left there to be rediscovered from time to time. Crunch.

Then one day, there was a collective 'enough is enough' feeling at the property. Wise men gathered under the trees and peered at the chipped and scraped boulder. Steel toe-capped boots tapped it and heels were dug into the grass to feel just how big it might be.

They lifted their eyes to the branches above their heads and confirmed that there would be a twisted mass of roots around the muckle steen and a big mechanical digger would probably rip them up and kill the old tree.

The muckle steen peeks though the lawn at Leith Hall (MAS)

A view of Leith Hall from the south east, 1907, by J. E. Hay (active early 20th century)

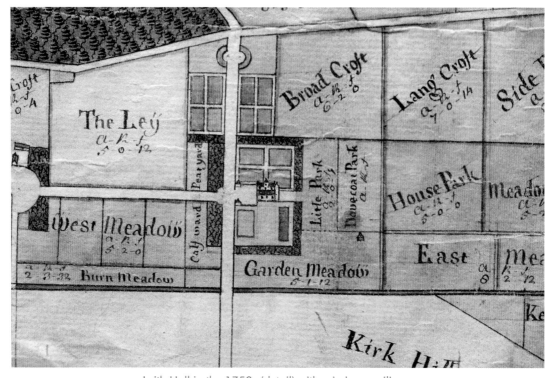

Leith Hall in the 1750s (detail) with missing pavilions

It would need to be dug out by hand and anxious expressions were shared at the task ahead.

Shannon the archaeologist got to hear about it and old plans and maps appeared with tiny images of little buildings just where the boulder was.

It was now 2007, when the old regional structure was coming to an end, and I was determined that some funds should be made available for research archaeology, a facet of conservation that was rarely indulged. The problem was always that there were no special funds for archaeology, unlike gardens, where buoyant dedicated accounts seem to overflow.

Shannon was convinced that there were pavilions under the lawn and always wanted to furtle about to see. As the old region began to die I suggested that some of these garden funds might be used to remove this hazard, and given the location this should be undertaken by archaeologists. The funds arrived, the gardens folk raised an eyebrow that their money might go to archaeology and Shannon was right. A small pavilion or lodge was found and in the corner a curious feature—a small water cistern where the pipe arrangement ensured it was kept full and constantly refreshed. Could it be a bottle cooler for those warm summer evenings so common in North East Scotland? So far it remains a mystery, but the grass cutter can now keep the lawn as he would wish.

Leith Hall pavilion dig
(MAS)

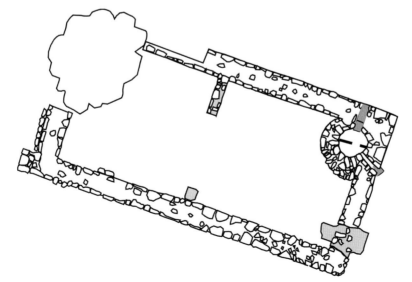

Leith Hall, pavilion plan (MAS)

23

CUSHIE DOO

A doo, or pigeon, whirled around the old steading buildings at Fyvie Castle, startled by the noise from the new car park next door. The factor, Mike, said, 'Look at that, the only bit anyone can see of the farm over the wall is that bloomin' doocot, and it's got a great big hole in the roof.'

It was 1984 and the castle was due to open the following summer, so after we got the money into a project account we arranged for a visit from the local slater, Alistair from Inverurie, whose family business, John Rhind and Son, had been repairing the roofs of Aberdeenshire for over a century. He was accompanied by Norman from Alexander Duguid and Son of Oldmeldrum, who ran a joinery business from the former livestock market buildings at the edge of the old county town. Oldmeldrum lost that status when the railway from Aberdeen went to Inverurie a few miles away and since then the town has experienced a genteel stagnation, mitigated by the presence of the local distillery turning out Glen Garioch single malt.

The three of us stumbled through a rotten door to what had been the apple store, where wizened, dried and barely recognisable ancient apples sat on slatted shelves

The doocot before repairs, 1984

Holes in the doocot roof, 1984

The Old Home Farm after the doocot roof was repaired

179

covered in dust and pigeon droppings. We waded through nettles tall enough to tickle our chins, and over piles of tattie pallets to the pend under the doocot, or dovecote, which sat high in the air under a pyramid-shaped slate roof as part of an elegant eighteenth century set of farm buildings. The whole place would have to be repaired, but even back in the 1980s it would cost hundreds of thousands of pounds, so it had to wait, at least until the castle was repaired and open to the public. It is still waiting.

We strode about, tramping down the weeds until we could get a decent view. Looking up into the roof, the underside was just visible. Alistair and Norman spotted that the boards, or sarking, under the slates were huge and that the rafters had been untouched for nearly two hundred years.

'Well, Norman,' I said. 'This will be fun. I will need you to get boards to match that and I want scarf joints on the rafters.' That meant that the timbers would be repaired

Norman Duguid's team repairing the doocot

John Rhind slaters repairing the doocot roof

Joinery work in progress, 1985

John Rhind slaters finishing the doocot roof

180

Nettles high enough to tickle your chin (IMD)

with new ends spliced on, rather than bolted at the side as would often be the way in any old roof not belonging to the Trust.

'Oh aye,' he replied. 'Nae bother.' He was getting used to me after a few earlier escapades. Alistair would have no difficulties doing what I had asked of him, and it looked pretty straightforward for the slaters.

A few weeks later up went the scaffolding and over we went to see what was happening. We stood looking at the collapsing roof and Alistair said, 'I've never seen onything like that before.' The massive slates were shiny and smooth with hardly any patination. 'Fit would make them like that?' As we got down, a pair of cushie doos quickly circled and made for the holes in the roof, first trying to land on the slates, their claws scrabbling about trying to get a grip and polishing them. 'Ah,' we said in realisation.

24

FOGHORN

There was a time when it was thought that a good number of my Trust years might be spent in the Broch up on the Buchan coast. Bill, the area surveyor and assistant director, called one day. 'Ian lad, could you pop up to Fraserburgh and have a look at the lighthouse? We might be taking it on.'

A day or two later I drove into the town. The streets were empty of people and litter. 'Douce' was the word that sprang unbidden to mind. Each house seemed to be built without front gardens from blackish grey granite, the buildings echoing the sky. There was no one to ask the way, so I peered down the streets and over the slated roofs until Kinnaird Head lighthouse appeared in the distance. I drove slowly through the narrow streets to the cliff top. The air blowing in through the car vents brought the unmistakable

Kinnaird Head lighthouse (IMD)

Foghorn pipes at Kinnaird Head lighthouse (IMD)

whiff of long-dead fish and decaying seaweed. Small sheds were dotted about where local fishermen stored their gear and some sold the catch to the locals. Most of the fisher folk had long since moved away from the older parts of the Broch, often into very well-appointed houses elsewhere. Fishing at the time could produce an affluent population.

Kinnaird Head lighthouse was being mothballed and the last keeper was retiring. All around the ground nearby were old nets and buoys. The old chap, as he seemed to me at the time, opened the door. This lighthouse was inside a tower house and the Stevenson family had built the cylindrical column right up through the stone vaults to let the top with the glazed lantern pop out of the roof. Each room and stairwell was painted in that thick glossy manner that you find in army barracks where time is passed in never-ending maintenance and painting walls seems to be a good winter occupation.

The spiral stair twisted up, passing offices, toilets and kitchens that were beginning to take on an air of abandonment. Yellowing notices were pinned to the walls and cobwebs furnished the corners of the windows. Up at the top, the multi-faceted lenses stood unmoving and the massive bulb was no longer needed. We stood there, puffing slightly after the climb, looking out to the sea, which stretched away in grey stillness, merging seamlessly with the sky. Around the foot of the castle, the weathered grass struggled in wind-flattened clumps. Snaking across from the foot of the tower to the cliff

A lighthouse within an ancient tower house (IMD)

Trumpet at the cliff edge (IMD)

edge was a large pipe. We descended the tight, winding stair and stepped out into the breeze. It has been suggested that if the wind in Fraserburgh ever stops, the people will fall over, and it was certainly brisk that day.

The pipe turned out to be the conduit from the pump house to the foghorn. I stumbled over the tussocks and there it was, ending at the cliff edge with a huge trumpet, a bit like the horn of an ancient gramophone, on which a little dog might listen with its head cocked to His Master's Voice. Any wee dug doing that here would have found itself flying over the waves far below as the great *parp* sounded.

Acquiring the lighthouse looked as if it might be the last hurrah of the departing CEO, who was due to retire in a few months' time. Even as a lowly surveyor, I could hear the rumble of dissent from the top as the Edinburgh management wondered why they should acquire a disabled foghorn on the edge of the world, as they viewed it from the beautiful south. The weeks and months rolled slowly by and it seemed as if a decision would never be made until he was gone, and when the time arrived, as if by magic, the Trust withdrew and the local council took over and did an absolutely splendid job of caring for the old place. The yard is tidy and a tearoom looks through large windows onto the steel-coloured sea with the fishing boats rocking and pitching as they make their way in, laden with fish. There is still a whiff of the docks about the place, thank goodness.

25

BANG

Late one afternoon I was sitting in the stables at Castle Fraser, my office window open, and as the afternoon drew to a close there was a distant crack and the electricity flickered. I wandered out and looked down the hill to see smoke rising from an electrical transformer high up on a pole next to the castle. I took a stroll down to see what had happened and found, in the castle courtyard, a marquee. 'What's that doing there?' I thought and stepped inside. Looking around me I saw that the canvas was held up by a steel frame and that at each post was a big steel pin, one of which had gone through the mains cable when it was driven into the ground. The young and well-trained Property Manager had risk assessed the placing of the tent, but the cables it seemed were not where they were supposed to be, placed there decades earlier before the Trust arrived by long gone technicians. Although I knew that the power was off, I looked at the network of steel around me and the pin in the ground and felt a rush of adrenaline as my hands tingled and my heart raced. Images came unbidden to mind of me with smoke rising from my hair.

Marquees had become quite a challenge for the conservation team in the early 2000s. The Trust had to find new income and marquee events were popular. Acres of white canvas would appear on the lawns and bonnie brides would trip into their blissful partnerships in the shadow of the great houses. Who could resist?

One of the first marquees was the venue for an oil industry event way back in 1983, when Marathon formally opened an oilfield from the biggest tent anyone had ever seen, in the field next to Castle Fraser and we ensured far away from electric cables or water pipes. Hundreds gathered and flash cars overwhelmed the car park. In the days before the big event, scruffy men and women from the BBC emerged from their vans with clipboards in hand, burying cables to transmit the event live, but no one thought what might lie below the turf as it was dug up.

As the years rolled by Castle Fraser became less popular with the marquee folk and Haddo House, with its quietly spoken Marchioness, 'whispering' Lady June Aberdeen, became popular with Total for their annual staff ball. A title can be a bit of an asset for the brand. These were the boom times in the North Sea oil industry, which brought big

Fireworks over Fyvie Castle (Neal Murray Photography)

bucks to the shire, though at Haddo this would support the musical aspiration of the Marchioness and her opera society, rather than the Trust.

After the Oilies had danced the night away and climbed back into their Aston Martins and their glasses were gathered and washed, Lady A. would commandeer the marquee for her gala night. Usually, this would be hosted by star guests such as Ronnie Corbett. Wee Ronnie arrived one dreich October day and was taken up to his room among the display rooms on the top floor, a tiny suite to match his stature, and he was none too pleased. The room was rather tired and worn, with frayed bedspreads and threadbare tassels hanging from the half tester bed. He was not mollified with what was described as country house chic.

Those gala nights were for the county set and music-loving farmers. Amateur thespians would gather with the tweedy gentry and the Volvos from the farms would vie with Subarus from the big houses to get the best parking spots away from the mud.

In later years, Fyvie Castle would steal the crown for most marquee-friendly property. Robert, the effusive manager from Pitsligo, or some other chilly corner of Buchan, schmoozed the oil company executives and gigantic tents would overwhelm the castle, well away from any risk from hidden cables. His brand of stylish couthiness seemed to trump the title. He had once been the manager of Haddo's music and dramatic society where his perjink persona worked wonders. I asked him once if I might use the word 'perjink' to describe him and he burst out laughing. It can mean neat, tidy or smart, but it can also mean rather strait-laced, and that's not oor Robert.

When he came to the Trust, he eventually ended up in the pink palace that is Fyvie Castle. The old place can seldom have seen so many parties and parades as it has during Robert's tenure. Vintage vehicles fill the lawn on summer days, antique fairs abound and pipe bands, weddings beyond counting and music are quite a common occurrence. But the stars of the Fyvie show were the oil companies.

Marquee at Fyvie Castle

Marquee anchors pounded into the lawn

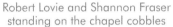
Robert Lovie and Shannon Fraser
standing on the chapel cobbles

Shannon Fraser, Trust Archaeologist

Through the summer when these giant marquees were squeezed safely into the grounds, pop stars would blast out their tunes and the glass would rattle in the castle windows. On the nights when the party budget was matched by a high price per barrel of oil, light shows would fill the sky with colour and fireworks cracked and boomed so loudly that they could be seen and heard twenty miles away. After a while, the conservators' anxieties began to be heard, especially when one windy night a tent flap lifted a giant pin out of the ground, whacking it on the castle walls, fortunately to little effect.

Everyone knew that something had to change and soon the marquees were relocated away from the castle and into the field nearby. Robert used his schmoozing skills on the tenant farmer and the fences were removed, power cables and water run in and we had a look under the grass.

The historians tell us that Fyvie appears in the records as far back as the reign of the medieval king William the Lion. It now stands in a picturesque landscape

Gardens and a chapel under the turf at Fyvie

| Assumption of Mary | Resurrection of Christ in a form that dates back to the middle ages | Woman of the apocalypse standing on a crescent moon and crowned with the stars (damaged) |

All the carvings are possibly from Seton's chapel (IMD)

of the nineteenth century but there is a depth of time there that has left its mark and is waiting to be uncovered.

The Trust archaeologist led the way and with colleagues from the archaeological community found what could be the family chapel or a summerhouse. As the turf was peeled away, just a few millimetres below the grass, a cobbled floor and remnants of wall foundations appeared. They scraped away the soil and small finds were turned up, including window glass which was later dated to the occupancy of Alexander Seton, seventeenth century Chancellor of Scotland and first Earl of Dunfermline. What, we all wondered, was this wee building for? Robert, scion of Buchan farmers looked at the cobbles and suggested, 'It looks a bittie like a wee stable'. Others thought it might have been a chapel rather than a tea house, or perhaps a private study.

The full story of the investigation will one day be told and will rewrite the history of not only Fyvie but so much more, and working alongside the archaeologist has been truly eye-opening. There are stories of lost gardens and of the decorative stonework high on the castle, which answer some queries I have not had the nous to work out for myself.

Curiously, if you peer around a corner into a small room overlooking this lawn there is a small collection of carved images. Could they be rare survivals from the chapel? Here you will find a crucifix, a spectacularly detailed resurrection in a form that goes back to the Middle Ages, a figure representing the Assumption and a curious 'horned' Mary, which may be a representation of Revelation 12:1: 'And there appeared a great wonder in heaven; a woman clothed with the sun, and the moon under her feet, and upon her head a crown of twelve stars'.

As I walked around the castle way back in the 1980s, my eye was drawn to three stone panels on the walls. They were unlike anything I had seen before. One was a curious figure, its hands awkwardly placed as if to maintain its modesty, even if the areas of immodesty were not quite where they should be. The other two were portraits. One of the subjects wore a pointed hat and the other a turban. The latter I called 'the Moor'; I think I had just watched Charlton Heston as El Cid. All three were damaged, as is much of the other decoration on the castle walls and roof, and they are now part of a major programme for repair.

Today everyone is particularly worried about the strangely modest character. It has been coated with something like paint and is slowly disintegrating. Soon the detail will be gone forever and the recent analysis is most timely. It seems not to be what so many have thought. Rather, it is likely to be the remains of an image of a water carrier and the head is a vase. When explained by the archaeologist it becomes so obvious. It would have been once embedded in the garden wall, as would the other two. The Moor is not in fact an adversary of Charlton Heston; it is Khair ad-Din Baba Oruç (better known to us as Barbarossa), admiral of the Turkish fleet under Suleiman the Magnificent, and the chap in the pointed hat is Pietro Lando, Doge of Venice. There is little doubt that the insight Shannon Fraser has brought to the significance of Fyvie and many other of the great houses in Aberdeenshire is revolutionary. Her many publications have developed our perception of the sophistication and grandeur of these renaissance houses with a rigour previously unseen and her departure form the Trust and Scotland in 2016 is a loss that will be hard to recover.[8]

Every year slaters take a look at the roof when the leaves fall and the gutters are cleaned and those statues are inspected by eye to see if they need a little tender care.

Bowler playing pétanque

Musician playing a shawm
(Graciela Ainsworth Conservation)

Statue of a trumpeter

Aquarius the water carrier

Khair ad-Din Baba Oruç

Pietro Lando, Doge of Venice

(Graciela Ainsworth Conservation)

The slaters who clean the gutters are, to a man, local to the shire and often from a Peterhead firm.

Peterhead is not to be confused with its near neighbour, Fraserburgh, though both are fishing towns on the Buchan coast. The local language is a particularly impenetrable form of Doric, itself a dialect that challenges the non-local, but the locals will usually try to modify it for us foreigners. 'Aye well,' they will say. 'It's a bittie blustery, but we'll just about manage, ye ken.'

Sometimes I have gone up on the roof with the slaters to have a look at the little statues, standing there in their period costume. Some are playing musical instruments while others seem to be well-dressed gentlemen or nobles playing bowls, in the underhand manner of pétanque, a French sport restricted to the gentry and forbidden to commoners from the fourteenth to the seventeenth centuries.

The oldest of these wee men can look a little naïve, with their elongated bodies and their arms held awkwardly on their hips in a gesture used in portraits of the time to suggest action and swagger, or because the pose shows off their expensive silk sleeves. The long bodies might be explained by the foreshortening effect of looking up at them.

Robert called one October day in 2015. 'Ian, you jist would not believe it,' he said in a refined Doric. 'Ane of the stones has fallen into the courtyard.'

The assistant surveyor went over and sure enough there was a block of red sandstone, about the size of a shoebox, in the office. It was from the 1890 clock. We initiated a major inspection, with hoists and masons, engineers and conservators pushing and pulling on every stone.

First, though, we had to raise a protective fence, just in case another stone should fall. It was not a lovely National Trust fence with a tasteful colour and maybe some interpretation; there was no time for that. A muckle metal fence appeared and prospective brides could be seen swooning as their big day loomed and they could see that their photos would be ruined.

The engineer standing in a basket on a hoist would grab the body of each statue and give it a shake, pushing in lead wedges as a temporary stabilisation when necessary. At one point while standing 30m in the air he gave one of these wee men a shoogle and decided it was doing well, so reassuringly patted it on the head, which came off in his hand, decapitated and soon to be labelled and placed in a box. As the first wedding drew near, the nervous bride arrived to look around and he could see from his hoist up on the castle roof that she was rather worried. Down he came, striding purposefully over to her in his hard hat and high-vis jacket . 'Don't you worry,' he said. 'We will get this fence away. I do this kind of inspection all the time and there will not be any problem.' True to his word we were able to have the castle ready for her big day. These little events are usually unseen and unknown, but they reflect the care and humanity that I always find in the men and women who care for these places.

Working closely with Graciela Ainsworth Conservation, architect Dave Chouman and the Trust archaeologist Shannon Fraser, the report was completed and a preliminary analysis revealed that the stonework was not only precarious but precious—probably the finest array of Scottish renaissance and later sculpture anywhere. It is a rare treasure. The cost of repair is huge and will need the effort of all concerned to push it on. I hope that the project will not take the time it took for Craigievar to be repaired. The stonework will not last that long. Fyvie will need a champion and I am sure that the staff are up for the challenge.

26

SKIRLIE

Nicky Tams were legendary apparel in the shire. While I never saw them worn in anger, so to speak, they would be a part of the national costume of the Garioch, were it to be independent. The locals are happy to take a joke at their own expense and their love of neeps is legendary. Oats too. It is said that what others feed their livestock we treat as a delicacy. 'Aberdeenshire: Powered By Neeps' should be the motto. The cuisine of the North East is developed from the land that produces it and on occasion is startlingly unsophisticated, if delicious.

When I lived at Haddo in those early days in 1983, I would travel into the local village for sustenance and on a Thursday night, blessings from above, a fish and chip van would be in the square. It was ancient, painted in that pastel blue so popular in the 1950s, and had been converted by the enterprising fryer. The lum stuck up through the roof, sending fatty fumes into the night air. The thing was run by a husband and wife now getting on in years. He appeared to be an ageing teddy boy, known to all as Greasy Dod.

Sitting at the side of the village square was the shop, and this is where I first came across the buttery or rowie—the local version of a croissant, only flat, round and leavened with lard—on my first Aberdonian Saturday. As a Glaswegian I had grown up eating morning rolls. These delicacies are a great treat and look like any other roll, except they are chewy with a delicious crust. So when I asked for rolls at the shop and was handed these flat things I thought they had failed to rise and I had been had.

Big Doug was the manager at Pitmedden garden, a garrulous and cheerful man with the raconteur's ability to weave tales. He loved an audience, and I would regularly be asked to visit in the morning. His motivation was to share his tea break—the fly cup, as the locals call it—and to sneak in his favourite snack of toasted butteries with Stilton. He was known as Big Doug for a reason.

It was Doug who had introduced me to The Dairy, a wonderful institution in Inverurie. The main grocers shop has since had a makeover and is rather swish, but the adjoining restaurant remains resolutely unchanged. The kitchen, which is visible to all, is staffed with local folk, brosie quines and sturdy dames. The food is a delight of North East

Inverurie war memorial (IMD)

fare—stews and sausages, pies and peas, and without doubt the best skirlie anywhere. 'Skirlie, what's that?' Oatmeal, onion (ingin in the dialect) and fat, at a seriously unhealthy ratio.

Inverurie was a nice provincial wee place in 1983 when I first saw it. The marketplace was filled with local shops, chemists, grocers and ironmongers. The latter had been there for generations and still sold nails, buckets, door handles, paint and fireguards at the back, while at the front it did a roaring trade in the sale of ceramic dogs looking pitifully up at ancient owners, or small porcelain children jumping in puddles. There would be picture calendars with images of Scottie and Westie dogs and plates decorated with tartan rims. They seemed quite popular. It was not a tourist town so they all went to the locals. The owner usually wore a kilt.

Wearing the kilt in Inverurie or any other part of the North East is not all that common on a normal working day, though the sight of a chap wearing one would not cause a second glance. In the Glasgow of my youth, however, wearing a kilt meant social death and maybe a good doing (beating). In the North East things were different, though there was a hint of *The White Heather Club* about the dances held in the village halls.

I discovered at these hops the curious cultural norm that the dance music of east and west coasts have a subtle difference. In the west the accordion is played with a loose fervour befitting the land of the Gael, while in the east a strict tempo is observed, born of a desire for order and etiquette. A perjink and proper approach, it is Jimmy Shand versus the Red Hot Chilli Pipers. Accordions and bagpipes were the musical instruments of the Garioch, with the fiddle following closely behind.

Pipe bands are still a feature of the Aberdeenshire cultural scene. In the 1980s every town would have one and they were often linked to the British Legion so had a militaristic shade to them, usually diluted by young people learning the thing. The drum major struts his stuff at the front but the one to watch is the pipe major. That's the real leader; standing at the front of the parade of pipers, on the right, he keeps the band together with a nod, a wink and the exaggerated stamping of a foot.

The Pitmedden gardener and I were in the local band and he balanced the big bass drum under his cheery face, marching with a slight swagger as the

The author on his way to the pipe band with Finn the Gordon setter

sticks maintained a steady beat. I had started piping late in life, at twenty-three, and while looking the part I was a weak player, so I was usually hidden in the middle of the ensemble among the school kids to obscure the misplaced squeals and missed notes I produced. Each November on Remembrance Day we would parade at the front of local groups to the war memorial. Stepping out in front of scouts, cadets, badminton players and on one occasion pink tutu-ed baton twirlers, we assembled at the granite statue in the marketplace.

Every year the ceremony follows the same pattern. The square falls silent as a piper plays 'Flowers of the Forest'. In between there is an opportunity for the players to gaze around at the old houses and shops. The assembled community groups deliver wreaths and plant their paper poppies in the grass. The memorial, like every other, is covered in names, listed by regiment. Eventually you begin to count and it immediately becomes clear that the World War I names vastly outnumber those from World War II.

World War II is by far the war we hear most about. It is in the movies and on the curriculum, and until recently the old soldiers were still around. What must the effect of World War I have been on this community? The loss of so many young men devastated farming, fishing and industry, emptying homes and taking the birth of a generation that should have followed.

This devastation had a minor effect on the Trust decades later, and in its own way is desperately poignant. 'Where does all this holiday cottage furniture come from?' I asked the curators.

'Well, some lovely old Nellies leave it,' they told me, referring affectionately to the ladies of Edinburgh who donated to the Trust in their wills. They were the World War I generation who stayed unmarried in a world without enough men, leaving no heirs.

When the wreath laying is finished, the band strikes up a jolly tune and heads for the church, and soon it is all over for another year.

27
LOWSIN TIME

Staff in the Trust were once categorised by their occupation as either Lilies or Boots. The curator types were the Lilies, as they were thought to flounce around in a rather effete manner making things look nice. Meanwhile the Boots were the gardeners and estate managers who strode about in the wind and mud keeping the place green and profitable.

Curiously they dressed similarly, with the difference in their uniform being largely one of colour.

Each would wear a lot of tweed. Their footwear tended to be sturdy brogues, and corduroy was a favourite for the breeks. For the Boots there were a lot of earth tones—Lovat greens, burgundy and fawn, and their shoes were usually heavily built with treaded soles.

Mr and Mrs Will Marjoriebanks of that ilk with George Barron, the head gardener

Meanwhile the Lilies wore tweed of a pastel hue, bright yellow and crimson were always popular and the footwear was polished to a high mahogany gloss. This all began to fade when people like me arrived who seemed to have a foot in both camps.

I was, I suppose, a Lily in Boots.

As a strange hybrid, walking in both realms, I was well placed to observe and sometimes participate in the enthusiasm of each. I could see and benefit from their insight and the wrinkles in their personalities. So it is that these stories have tried to capture a little of the essence of those men and women who are the unseen champions who protect our castles. Many of those I have mentioned are gone, though not all.

Scotland's heritage lies not just in the buildings and the countryside, but also in the people who live here and the lives they lead. I was reminded of this shortly before my time with the Trust drew to a close. One day I looked around me to see to my side a bearded islander. Nearby was the old man of the mountains who is the greatest expert

A lily in boots, the author and a friend at Drum Castle (Dr Alison Burke)

on the Cairngorm massif, and beside him was a former executive of the *Press and Journal*. A wee dog hustled by on its way to a worn-out seat by an ash-covered stove. I was in a cluttered antique shop on Deeside and the owner handed out coffee in mismatched chipped cups, knocking over a pile of ancient magazines as his tatty tweed jacket caught the corner. In the background a tinny radio played 'Waltzing Matilda'. I will miss all of this when I go, I mused.

Those who have left us have, however, been replaced by new characters who bring their own personalities and skills to these places. They are different from those who have gone before but only in their experiences. They are people, and people never really change.

So the foibles of the past continue in new forms and new stories are being lived as I write. The biggest change we witness today arises from how heritage is viewed by those who visit, fund and manage it. Today more than ever, these are places to explore, exercise, shop, eat and photograph. Each generation of managers believes it has discovered something its forebears had overlooked and with a little effort a pot of gold will be revealed. That's fine. It was always this way and these places will continue to be reinvented to meet the needs of the current generation. I welcome this.

Around five o'clock on the 25th of April 1983 I was wandering back to the car park at Pitmedden where my first day was drawing to a close. One of the gardeners, Margaret, a lady of some maturity, caught my eye. 'Well, loon, lowsin time is't?' I smiled and raised a muffled 'huh?'.

On the 16th of December 2016 the National Trust for Scotland and I decided to part company, thirty-three years, seven months and twenty-one days since I walked into Pitmedden House to meet the team, Dick, Mike, Marjory and Flora. It was quite a journey and I am grateful for it.

Ian Mitchell Davidson
Aberdeenshire
2017

SELECT BIBLIOGRAPHY

Bain, Susan, 'Everyday Life on the Mar Lodge Estate' in *National Trust for Scotland Archaeology Bulletin No. 16* (Edinburgh, 2001)

Colvin, Calum, *Ossian: Fragments of Ancient Poetry* (Edinburgh, 2003)

Davidson, Ian M., *The Gargoyles and Cannons of Craigievar Castle* (Edinburgh, 2011)

—— (ed.), *Caring for the Scottish Home* (Edinburgh, 2001)

Dingwall, Christopher, *The Hermitage: An Historical Study* (Edinburgh, 1995)

Dingwall, Christopher, Don Aldridge and Patrick Eyres, *The Hall of Mirrors: Reflections on the Sublime and on the Iconography of Ossian at the Hermitage, Dunkeld* (Leeds, 1999)

Forbes-Sempill, Sir Ewan, *Aul' Days: The Family of Corse and Craigievar* (Aberdeen, 1984)

Gow, Ian, *Craigievar Castle* (Edinburgh, 1999)

Fraser, Shannon, 'Exploring the Duke's Pleasure Ground at Dunkeld', in *National Trust for Scotland Archaeology Bulletin No. 17* (Edinburgh, 2001)

—— Ritual marks found at Pitmedden and Craigievar', in *National Trust for Scotland Archaeology Bulletin No. 21* (Edinburgh, 2003)

—— 'Leith Hall makes a grand entrance', in *National Trust for Scotland Archaeology Bulletin No. 27* (Edinburgh, 2007)

—— 'Drum's Lost Gardens Revealed', in *National Trust for Scotland Archaeology Bulletin No. 28* (Edinburgh, 2008)

Geddes, Jane, *Deeside and the Mearns: An Illustrated Architectural Guide* (Edinburgh, 1991)

Jamieson, Fiona M., 'Mar Lodge Estate, Vol. 1, Documentary Research', cited by permission (1998)

Learmont, David, and Graham Cuthbert, *Drum Castle: Aberdeenshire* (Edinburgh, 1977)

Linklater, Eric, *The Music Of The North* (Aberdeen, 1978)

Macpherson, James, *Fragments of ancient poetry, collected in the Highlands of Scotland* (Edinburgh, 1760)

McKean, Charles, *Banff and Buchan: An Illustrated Architectural Guide* (Edinburgh, 1990)

Scott, Schomberg, *Crathes Castle* (Edinburgh, 1979)

McKean, Charles, *The Scottish Chateau: The Country House of Renaissance Scotland* (Stroud, 2001)

Royal Commission on the Ancient and Historical Monuments of Scotland, *Mar Lodge estate, Grampian: an archaeological survey* (Edinburgh, 1995)

Shepherd, Ian, *Aberdeen and North East Scotland (Exploring Scotland's Heritage)* (Edinburgh, 1996)

Shepherd, Ian and Charles McKean, *Aberdeenshire: Donside and Strathbogie, an Illustrated Architectural Guide* (Edinburgh, 2006)

Simpson, W. Douglas, 'Fyvie Castle', in *Proceedings Of The Society Of Antiquaries Scotland Vol. 73* (Edinburgh, 1938)

Smiley, Lavinia, *The Frasers of Castle Fraser: A Scottish Family in the Nineteenth Century* (Wilton, 1988)

Stirling, A. M. W., *Fyvie Castle: Its Lairds and Their Times* (London, 1928)

Tranter, Nigel, *The Fortified House in Scotland, Vol. 4: Aberdeenshire, Angus and Kincardineshire* (Edinburgh, 1966)

Walker, David and Matthew Woodworth, *Aberdeenshire: North and Moray* (New Haven, 2015)

Walker, David, Joseph Sharples and Matthew Woodworth, *Aberdeenshire: South and Aberdeen* (New Haven, 2015)

USEFUL WEBSITES

Aberdeen Art Gallery www.aagm.co.uk

Aberdeenshire Council Archaeology www.aberdeenshire.gov.uk/leisure-sport-and-culture/
archaeology

Cairness House www.cairnesshouse.com

Calum Colvin www.calumcolvin.com

Cheong Fatt Tze Mansion Penang www.cheongfatttzemansion.com

Dame Evelyn Glennie www.evelyn.co.uk

Deeside Photographics www.deesidephoto.co.uk

Estonian Heritage Society www.muinsuskaitse.ee

Haddo House Choral and Operatic Society www.hhcos.org.uk

Historic Environment Scotland www.historicenvironment.scot

Institute of Field Archaeologists www.archaeologists.net

Inverurie Dairy www.mitchells-scotland.com

Inverurie Pipe Band www.inveruriepipeband.org.uk

Jim Henderson photographs www.crooktree.com

Lead Sheet Association www.leadsheet.co.uk

Little Houses Improvement Scheme www.nts.org.uk/Buildings/LHIS

Malacca Heritage Centre www.malaccaheritage.com

National Museum (Malaysia) www.muziumnegara.gov.my

National Trust for Scotland www.nts.org.uk

National Trust (Western Australia) www.nationaltrust.org.au/wa

Neal Murray Photography www.nealmurray.com

Penang Heritage Trust www.pht.org.my

Pipe Major William Hepburn www.thepipingcentre.co.uk/pipe-major-william-hepburn-senior

Rande Cook www.randecook.com

Rottnest Island www.rottnestisland.com

Royal British Columbia Museum www.royalbcmuseum.bc.ca

Royal Institution of Surveyors Malaysia www.rism.org.my

Scots Language Centre www.scotslanguage.com

Scottish Lime Centre www.scotlime.org

Scottish Natural Heritage www.snh.gov.uk

Society for the Protection of Ancient Buildings in Scotland www.spab.org.uk/spab-scotland

GLOSSARY OF ARCHITECTURAL TERMS

armorial: a full or partial heraldic achievement, which may consist of shield, helmet, mantling, wreath, crest, motto and sometimes supporters and decorations.

ashlar: an individual stone of square masonry, or a wall built of such stone. It can have very thin joints and the visible face of the stone may have a variety of treatments, including tooled or smoothly polished finishes.

bolection: a carved or shaped moulding that projects beyond the face of a panel or frame.

butt joint: two pieces of wood joined by simply placing their ends together without any special shaping.

harling: surface finish to rubble masonry, usually with a rough finish.

ogee: a curve shaped like an S, consisting of two arcs that curve in opposite direction, so that the ends are parallel.

pend: a passageway that passes through a building, often from a street to a back court.

rybats: the Scottish term for dressed stone at the side of a door or window when the surrounding masonry is laid in courses.

Sheela na gig: a figurative carving of a woman with exposed or enlarged genitalia.

starts: the Scottish term for dressed stone at the side of a door or window when the surrounding masonry is not laid in courses.

yett: a gate or grille of latticed wrought iron for defensive purposes. A royal warrant was required for their use.

REFERENCES

1   The Venice Charter for the Conservation and Restoration of Monuments and Sites was drawn up in 1964 and provides an international framework for the conservation and restoration of historic buildings.

2   From *Popular Rhymes, Fireside Stories and Amusements of Scotland*, published by W & R Chambers (1842).

3   Greig, Moira K., Excavations in the Laird's Hall, Drum Castle, Aberdeenshire; The Society of Antiquaries of Scotland, Vol. 134 (2004), pp. 423-456.

4   Greig, Moira K. et al, Excavations at Craigievar Castle, Aberdeenshire; The Society of Antiquaries of Scotland, Vol 123 (1993), pp. 381-93.

5   From the Manifesto of the Society for the Protection of Ancient Buildings, 1877, written by William Morris.

6   Child, Francis James, The English and Scottish Popular Ballads, 236A: The Laird o Drum.

7   MacInnes, Ranald, 'Rubblemania': Ethic and Aesthetic in Scottish Architecture; Journal of Design History Vol. 9, No. 3 (1996), pp. 137-151.

8   Fraser, Shannon Marguerite, 'To receive guests with kindness': Symbols of Hospitality, Nobility and Diplomacy in Alexander Seton's Designed Landscape at Fyvie Castle; Architectural Heritage, Volume 26, Issue 1, pp. 121-140.

The author reading *The Scottish Chateau* by Charles McKean, 2009